What Others Are Saying about
The Principle of Maximums

The *Principle of Maximums* offers a biblical and practical guide to experiencing abundance, contentment and joy as a manager of your God-gifted resources. Applying these principles will yield maximum returns of true riches.

Chuck Bentley, CEO, Crown Financial Ministries
Author of *Money Problems, Marriage Solutions*
Knoxville, Tennessee

Roger lifts managing money to a higher plane: from striving to have enough to strategizing with more than enough; from hoarding to generosity; from self-oriented to other-oriented; from fear to joy. With mathematical motivation and the witness of other writers, the author models the message of maximums that is biblical, practical, and life changing.

Keith E. Yoder, Ed. D., Founder and Minister
Teaching the Word Ministries
Leola, Pennsylvania

In this book, Roger Stichter repudiates the idolatry of self-sufficiency and the apathy that plagues much of contemporary Christian discipleship. He confronts the fear and the pride that cripples our response to life's opportunities and shrivels our witness. Stichter grounds his reflections in a careful engagement with the biblical text and blesses us with an extended invitation to a liberating stewardship based on the concept of "maximums" which he outlines in the text. His convictions and ideas are helpfully reinforced by intensely personal and vulnerably transparent narrative that describes the author's own practices and goals. The book offers abundant practical advice that will both challenge and guide intentional commitments to better steward our choices and resources at every stage of life.

The format of the chapters, with questions to consider and actions to take, ensures the usefulness of this text for Sunday School classes, Bible Study cohorts and discipleship groups wanting to think about stewardship from a Kingdom perspective. Full of wise counsel on how to live more freely and generously, Stichter's work is a gift to the Christian community. If we would risk paying attention and embrace his invitation to generous living, the witness of our churches will be strengthened by the holistic missional thrust and transformative potential of Stichter's gift to us.

Stanley W. Green, Executive Director
Mennonite Mission Network
Elkhart, Indiana

The Principle of Maximums by Dr. Roger Stichter reads like an autobiographical journey through years of faithfulness of handling money in a biblical fashion with "focus on eternity and not on things of this world."

This book weaves together Roger's formative years of family and local church experiences with his adult life as he shares insights on how to handle money in a biblical fashion.

The principles covered in the book are based on Scripture, and Dr. Stichter often goes directly to the text and regularly examines how Jesus approached these topics while ministering here on earth. I am so thankful to have Roger here at Grace teaching our students, and I pray that the Holy Spirit will use this book to teach and convict, even as it has in my own life.

Dr. Bill Katip, President
Grace College and Seminary
Winona Lake, Indiana

Roger Stichter has made a big impact on my life and in the lives of many of his students with his practical and sound financial principles combined with a biblical worldview. He brings those principles and perspective to *Maximums*, where he introduces a thought-provoking approach to living a life of purpose, contentment, and generosity. Roger's countercultural perspective on how we view and manage our finances strives to eliminate fear and bring financial peace of mind.

Jessica Bricker, CPA, Financial Advisor
Winona Wealth Management
Warsaw, Indiana

How much is enough? The inquiry is hardly new, but in today's commercial society, the question has a heightened relevance. Seeking to carefully address this, Dr. Roger Stichter has provided a thoughtful, convicting book that aims to liberate readers from the "financial strongholds" that slowly, and often unwittingly, bind us. Accessible in content, practical in approach, and orthodox in its application of Scripture—the book is a must read for people of faith desiring to accumulate treasure in the Heavenly realm.

Kevin Brown, Associate Dean, Associate Professor
Asbury University
Wilmore, Kentucky

Jacque Ellul, in his thought-provoking book entitled *Money & Power* suggests that the only way to profane the power of the God Money is through generosity. Roger Stichter has provided an insightful and practical guide for how to go about this calling for those of us who profess Jesus as Lord. I love his idea about maximums. It is simple yet profoundly helpful. I know Roger well and I respect how seriously he takes the concepts that make up this book. While helpful for any age, I am especially excited about the impact of his thoughts and concepts on a younger generation who is thinking critically about the use of their resources. A worthwhile read.

Dr. Kent Denlinger, Corporate Chaplain
Prasco Pharmaceutical Co.
Liberty Township, Ohio

Roger Stichter has written an easy-to-read but challenging book on how followers of Jesus can consider handling the difficult matter of money. As Jesus made clear, money is a god, and not a god to be taken lightly. It has powerful hooks into all of us that typically results in this powerful deity controlling us, drawing us away from our only allegiance to our Lord. Many books have been written on the topic of money and the Christian; Stichter's has the distinction of calling us to making choices to live with a "maximum"—a maximum amount of money that we choose to live with. He covers the basic categories in which we all spend money and urges us to consider limiting our spending, making choices that will free us from money's rule over us.

Jim Eisenbraun, Publisher
Eisenbrauns
Warsaw, Indiana

If we, as Roger lays out, embrace a life of *Maximums*, I have no doubt the impact will be overwhelmingly positive, not only this broken world but also our own lives. It's encouraging to know in some ways my family and I have been embracing this concept already, but even more exciting to catch a vision for what it would look like in several other areas. Much stress, overwhelm, and pain comes from thinking our minimum standard of living needs to be as high as others we see, yet setting a life of maximums gives the *freedom* we are really looking for, and it allows us to partner with God as He leads us towards the areas of highest impact He has for us.

Andrew Kipsey, CPA, Executive Pastor
Marina, California

Being one of Dr. Stichter's very first college accounting students, I was blessed not only to receive technical training from him, but also biblical wisdom for life and my future professional pursuits. I have been blessed by Roger again with the opportunity to read and provide a review of *Maximums*. The book is full of practical, biblical wisdom. In it, he not only explains the concept of *Maximums* but also provides practical application. Whatever your stage in life, you will find thought-provoking ideas based on what I will call true truth, or biblical truth. I was personally convicted about my own life and my perspective on money and possessions, including the example I set for my family. If God-honoring stewardship is important to you, I recommend you read *Maximums* to see how it might challenge you, irrespective of how you would rate your current level of obedience to God in this arena. I am grateful for a friendship with Roger that has spanned some 20-plus years. I pray that God will use Maximums to impact your heart and mind, as well as that of many others.

Jon Martin, CPA
Indianapolis, Indiana

Maximums is a must read for anyone who feels stuck in the cycle of consumption or hopelessly chasing the American dream. Roger Stichter offers practical, actionable financial advice for people in any stage of life. If you adhere to these principles, you'll experience true freedom as you seek to increase your standard of giving, not just your standard of living. I first encountered Roger's concept of *Maximums* while attending Grace College, and it's laid the foundation for how I view money and finances with a stewardship mentality. Read this book and you'll be challenged to contribute to the Kingdom instead of attempting to keep up with the Joneses.

Caleb Roth, Entrepreneur
Aurora, Colorado

Reading the concepts of "maximums" in this book has turned my thought process/philosophies around in my personal financial planning. These "maximum" concepts will allow my financial resources to be more abundant to build His Kingdom and my generosity muscle to be stronger.

Roger does a great job of describing the biblical concepts of money and the behaviors that hold us back in being generous. As he describes, fear is the primary behavior that restricts our willingness to give. But using Roger's concepts of "maximums" in all aspects of your lives will reduce the fear of not having enough and allow us to be more generous.

Lastly, Roger does a great job of taking his concepts of "maximums" and outlining practical ways to implement them throughout your life. If you can apply these concepts within your life, you continue to build your heavenly account not your bank account.

Wallace P. Wetherill, CPA, Managing Partner
BKD CPAs & Advisors
Fort Wayne, Indiana

Practical. Personal. Powerful. Setting and living by maximums will transform your life and help align your life with the purposes and priorities of Christ. The wisdom shared by Roger Stichter works. A life lived by the financial maximums suggested in this book produces joy, contentment and peace. Even more, the maximums put us in a position to give more, care actively and to invest our lives into the Kingdom of God. Seasoned by personal stories and insights, this book lays out the principles, the implications of living by the concept of maximums and makes the reader believe that she or he can do it.

Michael D. Wiese, Ph.D., Professor of Marketing
Fermanian School of Business, Point Loma Nazarene University
San Diego, California

The Principle of
MAXIMUMS

Living With Enough to Give Away More

The Principle of
MAXIMUMS

Living With Enough to Give Away More

Roger Stichter

P.O. Box 544
Winona Lake, IN 46590
bmhbooks.com
800-348-2756

The Principle of Maximums: *Living With Enough to Give Away More*
Copyright © 2019 by Roger Stichter

ISBN 978-088469-353-6 (print)
978-0-88469-355-0 (ebook)
BUSINESS & ECONOMICS / Personal Finance / Money Management

Published by BMH Books
Box 544, Winona Lake, Ind.
bmhbooks.com

Printed in the United States of America

Cover and interior design: Terry Julien

DEDICATION

To my Lord and Savior, Jesus Christ,
who I believe deserves all the credit
for the concepts in this book.

CONTENTS

ACKNOWLEDGMENTS

My wife, Jane, deserves a lot of credit for seeing this book come to completion. I have talked about many of the concepts of maximums written in this book for years but needed someone to tell me to finally write the book. My wife gave me space to do so through the many hours of time it took to research, write, and re-write. I am deeply grateful for her push and patience.

I thank Liz Cutler Gates and BMH Books for showing interest in my manuscript and providing encouragement. I have been blessed to work with a company so interested and involved in Grace College.

Jennifer Edwards, my editor, has been both encouraging and demanding. I needed both. It is a much better book because of her. Her ability to reorganize my thoughts into something much easier to read and comprehend was extremely valuable.

The people at Valley Springs Fellowship have been so supportive and encouraging during this process. Many of them listened to the questions I faced as I worked through concepts presented in the book and then gave needed advice. I'm thankful to be walking the Christian journey as part of such a church.

Thanks to those of you who were willing to read my manuscript and provide an endorsement. I know it took valuable time away from other activities and I appreciate your comments.

So many of the concepts in this book have been presented to the hundreds of students I have taught in the past twenty years. Without their encouragement, this book would not have been written either. It has been so encouraging to have past students tell me they are living by utilizing maximums in their financial lives. What a testimony to the fact that the concept of maximums works, and it can work for you, too.

Roger Stichter
Winona Lake, Indiana
January 2019

INTRODUCTION

Screwtape advises Wormwood in C.S. Lewis' book *The Screwtape Letters* that "prosperity knits a man to the World. He feels he is 'finding his place in it,' while really it is finding its place in him."[1] As Christian believers, how do we fight against the world taking a stronghold in our lives? We all know this is a possibility and often realize the world indeed does have a stronghold in our lives, but we struggle to know how to effectively combat it. This book is written to provide strategies for combatting the world's financial strongholds into the lives of Christ followers. Specifically, this book encourages using maximums—setting limits on how we will live out our financial lives to free up money for increased generosity.

In Philippians, Paul teaches that God keeps an account of our generosity. He tells the Philippians that God has credited their account based on their generous support (4:17 NIV). The accounting term "credit" is used when there is an increase in something owed. For example, if we deposit money into a bank account, the bank increases the amount it owes back to us by crediting our account. In some way, God also credits an account owed to us when we generously share what has been entrusted to us. Using money to buy ourselves more stuff does not increase the credit in our heavenly account, but being generous does (Mark 10:21). I believe most, and maybe all, Christians care about how large the credit is in their heavenly account, but the payout of that credit, however that will happen, seems so far removed from our current circumstances that we just don't put much thought into how that credit can be increased. The late Larry Burkett, one of the most respected Christian financial counselors and co-founder of Crown Financial Ministries, said, "Many Christians are going to be ashamed to face the Lord and explain why they hoarded money while others went hungry."[2] And in his book *The Treasure Principle,* Randy Alcorn reminds us of what Scripture tells us—our hearts go where we put God's money (Matt. 6:20).[3]

Being generous has the benefit of keeping our focus on eternity and not on things of this world. When we give money to help people instead of using it to buy more stuff for ourselves, it allows us to think about and pray for those people. In this way, we can focus on bringing the Kingdom of God into a hurting world.

So if the minimum biblical standard for giving is 10 percent (and I realize some will disagree with this percentage), why do Christians in the United States consistently give only about 3 percent of their income to the church? We are one of the wealthiest societies to ever inhabit the earth, yet many of us have failed to give even close to a tithe on our income. In *The Hunger Games* books and movies, the extreme indulgences of the wealthy and the seeming uncaring attitudes they have toward the poor who work hard to survive and supplement the lifestyles of the rich is shocking. But is the church in the United States really any different? The North American experience of wealth is an anomaly, but we strive to maintain our standard of living while being generally uncaring about the plight of the poor.[4] Author Ronald Sider says it this way, "By any objective criterion, the 4.5 percent of the world's people who live in the United States are an incredibly rich aristocracy living on the same little planet with billions of very poor neighbors."[5]

I believe that adopting a maximum lifestyle can increase the credit in our heavenly account, but it can also free us from greed. Once we establish how we will live, we will no longer need to continually strive after the next great thing we desire, freeing us to spend that energy in ways that will build the Kingdom. I believe we spend way too much time thinking about, researching, and saving to buy things we don't really need. And oftentimes we fail to use much of what we have anyway. I am not exempt from such practices. But I am interested in what would happen if as a church we really learned to be content as Paul talks about in Philippians 4? Instead of spending so much energy and money on things we don't really need, we could be spending time and money on what others really do need. Think of the possibilities!

I love to fish and will admit to owning several fishing rods. Each time I think I "need" another fishing rod, I spend time researching which rod and reel combination will best meet my *perceived* need for another fishing rod. This can go on for weeks. While I typically don't make financial decisions quickly, generally a good characteristic, I can spend a lot of time and energy on such decisions—time that could be spent on investing in people and prayer. After I have finally decided on which rod/reel combination will best meet my perceived need, I buy. You would think that after spending so much time and energy on this decision, I would find great satisfaction and joy in having another fishing rod. But, invariably, there is a letdown when I realize I have yet another rod that I will use sometimes, but it really won't bring me satisfaction. And that is just when I buy a fishing rod! It seems the larger the financial decision we have before us, the more time and energy we spend on that decision and an even greater realization that the stuff we just bought will not satisfy us.

In the following chapters, we will explore what the Bible says about money. Since there are many books that already take an exhaustive look at this topic, I will only highlight specifically what Jesus and other New Testament authors say. Fear and money often seem to operate together, so we will explore how fear shapes the way we handle money.

Then, after an introduction to what living a life by setting maximums means, I will discuss the tithe and how it can free us from being so obsessed with money. I will walk through several different lifestyle areas where we can begin to apply maximums, including housing, vehicles, retirement, and many more. And, as many of us who want to give more money away struggle to know where and how much to give, I will provide suggestions on where to give along with some guidelines for giving. At the end of each chapter, I have provided questions to provoke you to think through your own financial life and where changes can be made. These would be terrific when used in a small-group setting as well.

My challenge for you is to consider living by this concept of maximums, the idea of setting limits, or a ceiling, on your lifestyle to become more generous. In this book, I will walk you through concepts and ideas that will help you begin spending less on yourself and investing more in the Kingdom. I wholeheartedly believe that when you apply maximums to your finances, you will find freedom in ways you may have never experienced before, God will credit more to your heavenly account, and you will usher in God's Kingdom in unexpected and sacrificial ways.

THINK AND DISCUSS

1. Think about your family when you were growing up. Did you know what your parents believed about generosity? Did your family ever talk about being generous?

   _____

   _____

   _____

2. Ask two other people their thoughts on being generous. One of these should be your spouse. In their thinking, what does generosity mean? Is giving time a substitute for giving money?

   _____

   _____

   _____

3. What concerns do you have when thinking about setting maximums, or ceilings, on your financial life? What fears do you have? What doubts?

   _____

   _____

   _____

LIVING IT OUT

1. Pray for God to give you an open mind about setting limits, or a ceiling, on spending in certain areas of your life—which areas does He whisper to you? What might that maximum look like?

2. Take a look at the "Recommended Resources for Financial Wisdom" on pages 133 and 134. Purchase or borrow one or two of the resources that you think might be useful to you at this stage of your life. Take three or four useful tips from each to apply to your life.

1.
BIBLICAL CONCEPTS OF MONEY

In three of the four Gospels, two stories are always told together. The first story is the one where the little children came to Jesus, but the disciples tried to keep them away. For some reason, the disciples must have thought their leader, Jesus, was too important to entertain children. In biblical times, children were not generally held in high esteem. We are told, however, that Jesus rebuked the disciples, stating that the Kingdom of God was made for "such as these"—the children the disciples just shooed away. In the Mark account of this story, we are given more context when Jesus states that unless we receive the Kingdom like children, we won't even *enter* the Kingdom (10:15). This seems significant.

Now the second story is about a rich man who wants to know what it would take to enter the Kingdom. From the Mark account, we see Jesus says essentially the same thing he had said in the previous story—that this rich man needed to become like a child. Then He lists some of the Ten Commandments—don't murder, don't commit adultery, don't steal, don't give false testimony, honor your father and mother, and love your neighbor as yourself. The man confidently professes to have kept all of these commandments since he was a boy (10:17–20); he thinks he was a shoe-in. But Jesus doesn't ask about *all* of the Ten Commandments. He leaves off numbers one through four and ten. The first four commandments seem to be the ones that any good Jew would have kept. No other gods before Me. No idols. Don't misuse My name. Remember the Sabbath. Those were a given. But the tenth commandment was not a given. *Don't covet;* the one thing he lacked (v. 21). This must have been the rich man's main problem. He loved stuff and wanted more of it. Jesus knew this and tells him that if he wanted to be perfect and have treasure in heaven, then he needs to sell his stuff and give the proceeds to the poor. But the man just couldn't make that big of a sacrifice and he leaves—sad.

It was here that Jesus says something radical to the disciples, "How hard it is for the rich to enter the kingdom of God!" (v. 23). In fact, it would be easier to shove a camel through the eye of a needle (v. 25). What? This becomes a little more understandable when we consider that every Jew believed the rich were wealthy because God's favor was on them. The rich were already a shoe-in for the Kingdom. So, then, why did the rich guy even ask? Was he just looking for confirmation that rich people were already in the Kingdom? Or was he bragging, trying to draw attention to himself?

Let's go back to what Jesus means when he says "eye of a needle" in verse 24. When Jesus says it was hard for the rich to enter the Kingdom, the disciples are shocked. So Jesus explains further—it is easier for a camel to get shoved through the eye of a needle than for the rich to enter into the Kingdom. I believe he really meant just that—the hole in a real needle, though some have speculated he meant the Eye of the Needle Gate, which was a small entrance to Jerusalem and, thus, it was difficult for anything large to make it through. But getting through could be done with difficulty. The disciples knew shoving a camel through the eye of a needle was impossible, and we all know they had that part right. It would take a miracle. "Then who can be saved?" they ask, just the question Jesus was waiting to answer. He says, "Getting people into the Kingdom, even the rich, was possible, but only with God" (v. 27, author's paraphrase).

Continuing, Peter speaks up, reminding Jesus that he and the other disciples had already left everything, which is exactly what Jesus had asked the rich guy to do (v. 28). I'm sure he wondered, "what then will there be for us?" (v. 27). But Jesus emphasizes the great gain that could be experienced in heaven and on earth when one left everything behind. This makes no sense, does it? We still don't know how it relates to children, and it is backwards from what is logical, or so it seems to us. But think of it this way—leaving everything makes us dependent on others. We can't easily take care of ourselves if we don't have reserves. Children are like this—dependent! They don't have the ability to easily take care of themselves. They rely on parents to do this for them. With these two stories, I believe Jesus is making this point—that unless we are willing to release our desire to be dependent upon ourselves and become dependent upon God, *we cannot enter the Kingdom.* So, how do we do it, then?

In the United States of America, this is easier said than done. David Platt, author of *Radical: Taking Back Your Faith from the American Dream,* says, "We stand amid an American dream dominated by self-advancement, self-esteem, and self-sufficiency, by individualism, materialism, and universalism."[1] Indeed, our culture fights against what Jesus taught. As Christians here, most of us probably live with "comfortable guilt."[2] Comfortable guilt is when we are aware we should and could give away more money to do good for others, but we are not motivated enough to make the sacrifices in our own lifestyles to do so. I believe Platt is correct. Most Christians in the United States are willing to live with the guilt of knowing they could be more generous but not willing to live without the luxuries our society affords us. This is the crux of the matter.

Andy Stanley writes in his book, *How to Be Rich,* how many people tend to get so absorbed in trying to get rich that they don't recognize they are already rich. When people can finally recognize they are already rich, then they are able to be good at being rich, which means they can become better at being generous.[3]

The Bible teaches us a lot about money. And I mean *a lot!* I won't take time here to cover everything, but I believe covering some important Scriptures from both the Old and New Testaments that teach some basic financial concepts will be helpful to understand God's intention for money. Let's start with Jesus, as His teachings give us a picture of God's heart.

JESUS' TEACHINGS ON MONEY

Choose Whom You Will Serve

In Matthew 4, Satan offers Jesus the world, but Jesus' response is that we should worship and serve God alone (vv. 8, 9). Later, in Matthew 6:24, Jesus says essentially the same thing—we cannot serve both

God and Money. We must choose. Either we serve something based in this world, or we serve someone who is concerned with more than this world. It is clear we cannot serve both.

Focus on What Will Last

Also in Matthew 6, Jesus goes on to say that we shouldn't worry about things in this life (v. 25), that pagans worry about such things (v. 31); instead, we are to seek the Kingdom of God and His righteousness first (v. 32). I believe the emphasis here is *worry*. We aren't to continually worry or fret or fixate about what we will eat, drink, or wear. When our main concern is about where we will eat out next or the next thing we want to buy, we are not thinking about the Kingdom—instead, our focus is on things that will not last.

Jesus warns us in Luke 12 that true life does not consist in how much stuff we have (v. 15). We need to be rich toward God instead of being so concerned about storing up for ourselves on earth. Immediately following this story in Luke, Jesus teaches on not worrying about what to eat and wear. When we set our hearts on pursuing our basic physical needs, we are missing something greater. The treasure we store in heaven cannot be taken away (treasure we give to the poor), but things stored up on earth (material possessions) can be stolen away. Our hearts follow our treasure, so if we treasure and store up things on earth, our hearts will be there, too. But if we store up things in heaven, our hearts will follow (v. 34).

Don't Be Deceived by Wealth

The parable of the sower shows how wealth can be deceitful (Mark 4). It is equated to a thorn that grows up and chokes out the word (the teachings of Jesus), making it unfruitful. Many of us probably know of people who were on fire for God until financial success seemingly caused a change in them. They began seeking more wealth instead of seeking the Kingdom with the same fervor they had before becoming wealthy.

Also in Luke 6, Jesus gives us a contrast between the poor and the rich. He says the poor are blessed (v. 20) and the rich are receiving their reward in this life (v. 24). Again, this would have been the total reverse of what the Jewish culture believed. Mourning and weeping, which is what it appears the rich will be doing later, is not what happens in heaven, but hell.

Rely on God to Meet Your Needs

Jesus praises the woman who gave all the money she had to the temple treasury even though she gave only a very small amount (Mark 12). Although wealthy people came and gave a lot of money, Jesus says the woman's two small coins were worth more. Why? Because she gives it all. Talk about being dependent on God! She just gives up everything and decides to depend on God to meet her needs. Somehow this attitude of total dependence on God seems to fit becoming like a child.

Pay Attention to the Internals

Jesus says what is inside us, our character, is more important than what we portray on the outside (Luke 11). He says the Pharisees are full of greed and, apparently, not adequately taking care of the poor because being generous to the poor would clean the inside (vv. 39–41). And giving a tithe doesn't seem to be the solution either. The Pharisee in Luke 18 gives the tithe, but his heart wasn't right. Internal attitudes and motives matter.

Jesus discusses what defiles us in Mark 7. After being challenged by the Pharisees because some of the disciples were eating without properly washing their hands, Jesus states that it is not what goes into your body that makes you unclean, but what comes out from the inside—the heart. In verse 22, he mentions greed as one of the things that defiles. That is because greed keeps our focus on earthly things, what we can buy and have in this life, and shifts our focus away from what really matters for eternity—living for the Kingdom of God.

Share Your Wealth with Others

It is interesting that in the parable of the banquet in Luke 14, the first two excuses people give about why they couldn't come to the banquet dealt with the things they had just bought—a field and oxen. This seems to fit really well with Jesus' warning about how being so consumed with things we can buy on this earth will keep us from the kingdom (vv. 16–19, 24). It doesn't seem to mean that having things is bad, because the father in the parable of the lost son in Luke 15 has a lot of wealth. He throws a party with some of it when his son comes home. He isn't so worried about accumulating more that he isn't willing to give up wealth for people (vv. 22–24).

Use What You Have for Good—Today

In Luke 16, Jesus tells a parable that is pretty difficult to understand. A manager is fired and begins to give a discount to the people who owe things to his previous boss. Jesus seems to praise this "dishonest" manager. That doesn't fit much of what we have learned about being honest. But the lesson appears to be one of generosity—that things of this earth are to be used to help people (v. 9). We have no guarantee that anything in this life will be here tomorrow. People sometimes lose everything when natural disasters happen. All they had is almost instantly gone with no way to get it back. But if we will use what we have to help people, we will have heavenly gain. Hoarding with the intent of helping in the future is misguided and uncertain. Jesus again reminds us that we can't serve both God and Money (v. 13 TNIV). One will reveal where our heart really is and the other will be secondary.

Help the Needy among You

In Luke 16, Jesus tells how a rich man neglected to care for a poor man who is right at his doorstep. The rich man doesn't get a second chance. In death, the poor man is rewarded and the rich man is sent to hell. The rich man has his chance but cared more about his own comfort than helping the poor (vv. 22, 23).

Also, in the parable of the talents, Jesus commends those who help the needy (Matt. 25). Obviously, to help the needy, we have to give something away that we could have used for ourselves—our time, money, talents. Jesus says, if you aren't willingly and actively helping the needy, you aren't part of the kingdom but facing eternal punishment (vv. 34–43).

Right Your Wrongs

Zacchaeus seems to get it (Luke 19). When meeting Jesus for the first time, Zacchaeus decides to right the wrongs he had done to others and gives half of all he has to the poor (vv. 1–10). I wonder how many people he had cheated and then gave four times that amount back to them? How much did Zacchaeus have left? Maybe not very much. Jesus gives him the highest commendation in verse 9, "Today salvation has come to this house, because this man, too, is a son of Abraham. For the Son of Man came to seek and to save the lost." Zacchaeus seems to get what the rich man in Mark 10 did not.

OTHER NEW TESTAMENT TEACHINGS

Real Faith Meets Needs

Paul and other New Testament writers have several things to say about money. There are good books that expound on these teachings, including *Neither Poverty nor Riches* by Craig Blomberg and *Jesus and Money* by Ben Witherington. According to Blomberg, both Paul and James believe that saving faith and transformed living went together.[4] Faith without helping those in need was not real faith. James 5:3 tells us that accumulating unused riches is hoarding and not the true purpose of financial gain. Living in luxury and self-indulgence is not the purpose of money (vv. 1–6).

We can draw some conclusions that the church body described in Acts 4 must have had wealthy people in it because they began selling property to help others in need. Acts 4:34 describes this event, saying that they gave to the point where everyone's needs were being met. Blomberg continues, "Interestingly, what does not appear in this paragraph is any statement of complete equality among believers."[5] Sider seemingly agrees, as he states, "The massive economic sharing of the earliest Christian church is indisputable."[6] The rich were not just hoarding to themselves while the poor had unmet needs.

The Rich Should Help the Poor

In 2 Corinthians 8, Paul seems to make a case for financial equality (vv. 13–15). If we take this passage by itself without any of Paul's other teachings or the history in Acts, it might lead us to say that the rich must sell off all they have so everyone is financially equal. But nowhere in Paul's teaching does he make that kind of statement. Jesus and the New Testament writers clearly state that the rich should help the poor. But only once, to the rich young man of Mark 10, does Jesus make a reference to selling off everything, giving it away, and then following Him. Paul does not mention selling everything and giving it all away; in fact, you will not find that written by any other New Testament writer, nor anywhere in the Old Testament. But Paul "does recognize that there are some extremes of wealth and poverty which are intolerable in the Christian community."[7]

It Is the Love of Money that Is Dangerous

Paul writes to Timothy that preoccupying ourselves with hairstyles, dress, and jewelry is not an appropriate lifestyle for the believer (1 Tim. 2:9). First Timothy 6 seems to be in direct opposition to those today who teach a "prosperity" gospel, which suggests that God wants all of us to be wealthy in this life. Indeed, wanting to get rich is a trap that leads to foolish and harmful desires and destruction. Paul says the love of money is a root of all kinds of evil (v. 10). Roots must be there for a plant to grow. Roots support and feed the plant. Roots provide life to the plant. In a similar way, the *love of* money supports, feeds, and provides life to all kinds of evil.

Godliness with Contentment Is Gain

John's writings about money and wealth have a similar focus. First John 3 states that if we have material possessions, know of someone in need, and fail to help them, we aren't displaying God's love. John points out in Revelation that Smyrnan believers are materially poor but spiritually rich, while Laodicean believers are materially rich and spiritually poor. According to Witherington, "In any case, the New Testament is very clear that the goal of the Christian life is not success or prosperity, but godliness with contentment, which Paul stresses is the greatest gain of all."[8]

This is not meant to be a complete discussion of every New Testament passage. From the teachings of Jesus and other New Testament writers, it becomes clear that excessive wealth, wanting more money, and spending it on ourselves, especially while other people don't have enough to meet their needs, is not biblical. There seems to be a great emphasis by Jesus and Paul that we are to be concerned with the poor—meeting their needs is important. If we don't do that, are we really a part of the Kingdom?

OLD TESTAMENT TEACHINGS

Many biblically-based financial books begin with the Old Testament teachings on money. This book purposefully looks at the Old Testament last. If we believe part of Jesus' mission on earth was to help us understand the heart of God better, we must view all Old Testament teachings on money through what is understood from Jesus and other New Testament writers. John Piper helps us understand this better in *Living in the Light*, "The first commandment is, No other gods before me. Nothing in your heart should compete with me. Desire me so fully that when you have me, you are content. And then the tenth commandment is, Don't Covet."[9] This seemed to be what was keeping the rich young man from the kingdom. No matter what else the Bible seems to be teaching, the first and tenth commandments are pretty clear about what is not allowed.

Mark Allan Powell, in *Giving to God*, points out that Isaiah 5 issues a stern warning that "accumulation of material things must not dominate one's life to the extent that one does not even use or enjoy what one has."[10] Isaiah writes how adding more houses and fields (possessions) can take us to the point where we are "living alone in the land" (v. 8). Isaiah 58 and Amos 2 point out that God takes notice when we oppress the poor. Proverbs certainly has passages praising faithful financial stewardship, and some even seem to praise the wealthy. The book of Ruth gives an example where the landowners who have more crops than they need help the poor. Ruth benefits from this when she is allowed to harvest the leftovers from the field. The overriding principle appears to be that accumulation of wealth without using it to help needy people is not God's heart. Wealth tends to either distract us or totally rip our hearts away from the call "to act justly and to love mercy and to walk humbly with your God" (Mic. 6:8b).

Excessive wealth and the pursuit of it is spiritually dangerous. Living life this way creates an attitude of self-reliance and not dependence on God. If we aren't careful, we become focused on what we want and not focused on how we can help others who have their basic needs unmet. We can become easily deceived and begin to spend money on things that won't last, instead of spending money on helping others, which brings an eternal, spiritual reward. Most of us in the United States are very rich when compared to the rest of the world, and we have a responsibility to help those with unmet needs, both in close proximity to us and those living in other countries. Having the attitude of caring for and helping the poor is the heart of God, which He rewards us for in heaven. But Christians in the United States struggle to be generous and help the poor. The next chapter explores the powerful emotion that hinders generosity.

THINK AND DISCUSS

1. Jesus talks a lot about helping the poor. In what ways have you or your family helped the poor?

_____

_____

_____

2. Do you feel like Jesus' teaching on money are attainable? Why or why not?

_____

_____

_____

LIVING IT OUT

1. Find a way to help the poor in your city. You could volunteer in a soup kitchen or find some other way to help those who don't have adequate money to live well.

2. Recruit other people to go with you to help the poor.

2.
HOW FEAR AFFECTS OUR USE OF MONEY

*"Both rich and poor people struggle with fear. Poor
people fear not having enough. Rich people fear losing
what they have. Being rich does not solve the problem."* [1]

When I first read this quote, it really hit me how much Christians in the United States struggle with what I think is the crux of a major issue when it comes to money—fear. I don't believe the authors of *Rich Dad, Poor Dad* are Christian believers, but they have this concept regarding fear right. We can all struggle with fear, which can keep us from God's perfect will for our lives.

We live in a society that continually teaches us to be self-sufficient. The "American Dream" is basically one of self-sufficiency. We want to accumulate more than our parents had and be able to provide for ourselves. This dream has helped create a very wealthy society but also has taken us away from an attitude of dependence on God. I teach at a relatively "young" Christian college. It is not yet one hundred years old, which is pretty young as colleges and universities go. The college's endowment is small, not nearly enough to sustain the college should times get really tough. I've often told students this is a good place to be—dependent on God to keep the college going. If God wants the college to keep operating, He will provide. If He doesn't want it anymore, we can't sustain it ourselves. In a way our culture doesn't really understand, dependence on God is a good thing. But I believe fear keeps us from being willing to be dependent upon God.

For example, let's consider the tithe, which we will cover in depth in chapter four. In Matthew 23:23, Jesus states to the Pharisees that they should even be tithing on the smallest of their grown spices.

Since Jesus' teachings never decreased Old Testament teachings, this story validates the tithe as a money principle that is still biblical. If tithing is the biblical minimum, why the struggle to tithe? I believe it often boils down to fear. We all know Scripture teaches us that fear is the opposite of trust. When we allow fear to take over, we aren't putting our trust in God, and we know this is wrong. But when it comes to our financial lives, our society (and often other Christians) teaches us to make sure we care for ourselves first. This takes the form of providing more than we need for ourselves and giving less than we could to those in need.

How do we know when we are struggling with fear in this area? As Christians, we are struggling with fear when we continually believe we don't have enough money saved even when financial calculators show we have plenty saved to provide for unplanned financial setbacks. Both the Old and New Testaments seem to encourage providing for ourselves. How else in Acts could Christians have enough to help others in need? But when we try to protect ourselves from every unplanned event, we are living in fear. There is a great difference between provision and protection. Most financial advisors state we should save up between three and six months of living expenses in an emergency fund. If once we have saved up six months of emergency funds we continue depositing to this emergency fund, we are probably being motivated by fear. As will be discussed more later, the church was established partially as a means of sharing with those in need. Without the relationships formed in church, we wouldn't know who needs help. The people in the church in Acts helped each other but could not have done so if they hadn't known who needed financial support to sustain life.

Let's also take a look at life insurance. I believe having some life insurance to help support your spouse and children, if you are a wage earner for your family, is a wise use of some money. There are different methods advisors use to determine how much life insurance you may need. I have been shocked over how large an amount of insurance is shown as "needed" by some calculators. Let's say such a calculator shows you need $1,000,000 of life insurance and you buy $3,000,000 of insurance because you can afford to do so. This is probably an indication you are acting out of fear. Your motive is based more on protection than on provision.

Or how about if your daughter or son needs a car to help make transportation to work or school easier on your family, and you buy them a Hummer to more adequately protect them instead of a smaller, more economical vehicle? This is also a good indication you are probably acting out of fear. Plus buying the Hummer will take money that could have been used to help those in need.

Andy Stanley in his book *Fields of Gold* discusses how fear affects our view of money. He writes these words, "When viewed from eternal perspectives, the thing to fear is sowing too little"; "We should only fear God not being involved in our financial lives."[2] Morris also speaks to this issue, "I have noticed that the people most under the influence of the spirit of Mammon tend to have the most fear about their money."[3] We know Jesus said we can't serve both God and money (Matt. 6:24). Money in this passage means mammon. We understand the word money better, so most Bibles use the word money instead of mammon.

When I teach on generosity, I often talk about the idea of stewardship. We are stewards of God's resources. While these resources extend to all of our lives and how we use the life God has entrusted to us, it includes finances. When Jesus tells the story of the man going on a journey and entrusting bags of gold to his servants, the servant who does not steward the money well has the money taken from him and is thrown out (Matt. 25). God expects us to be a good steward of the resources He gives to us.

When talking about stewardship, I often ask what our response would be if God asked us to sell everything and give it to the poor as Jesus asked the young rich man to do. I believe nearly all of us would say, "That's not good stewardship!" But wait! If we don't really own it anyway, is it up to us? Are we like children or more like the young, rich man? Can't God do what He wants with His own money? Maybe we don't trust God enough, and I realize giving all I had away would be a really, really big stretch for me. I think Andy Stanley was right when he writes, "We have no fear when we realize we are giving away someone else's money."[4]

21

There was one time in my life when I faced the reality that I might be asked to use all the financial resources I then possessed and have nothing left. Our fifth child, Rebecca, was diagnosed with multiple medical issues at birth, and I was driving to Riley Children's Hospital in Indianapolis to see her after she had survived her first surgery. It hit me pretty hard on my drive to Riley that our family may be asked to use all the money we had for the care of this little girl. In that moment, I knew I would gladly do so. It was a realization in that instant that God owned it all anyway, and if He wanted me to use His money to care for Rebecca, I would do that.

Larry Burkett was a faithful, Christian financial writer who had a very great and positive influence on many people before he died. When it came to fear keeping us from doing God's will, he writes, "There's a price to be paid for every compromise, especially to God's Word. That price is the loss of peace from God. Compromise at any level results in further compromise until finally the conscience is seared, and right and wrong are no longer distinguishable."[5] Are you struggling to find peace? Maybe fear has a greater stronghold in your life than you have believed.

Look, the truth is that many of us Christians live with some fear of the unknown. But if we must receive the kingdom of God like a child, then our trust in God will be greater than our fear of the unknown. I love the quote by Gary Moore in his book *End-Times Money Management* because it refocuses us outward instead of on our inward financial fears:

> The facts say that we are rich enough to fulfill the Great Commission to evangelize the world *and* the Great Commandment to love our neighbors as ourselves. Our hearts just need to be free of those feelings of economic fear and greed. And our lives need to be open to the spirit of plenty.[6]

Fear can be crippling. It is probably most obvious when someone physically can't move to avoid a dangerous situation. But fear can also financially cripple us. If you recognize that fear has a grip on you, get help. Continue to stand against fear in Jesus' name. Claim God's promise that He will never leave you or forsake you (Deut. 31:6). Get people to pray with you and for you. Read Romans 8 and realize that the mind set on what the flesh desires does not bring us the peace of God.

We have explored biblical concepts of money and how fear affects our use of money. The next chapter introduces the principle of maximums, which has the ability to conquer fear and allow you to use money in a biblical manner.

THINK AND DISCUSS

1. In what areas of your life does fear have a grip on you? Do you have someone to talk with about those areas?

\
\
\

2. Do you believe Gary Moore is correct that our society is rich enough to fulfill the Great Commission? Why or why not?

\
\
\

LIVING IT OUT

1. Find someone to talk with about your fears related to money.

2. If you realize your fear is deeper than just with the issue of money, begin seeing a Christian counselor to get help with identifying and conquering your fears.

3.
LIVING BY
THE PRINCIPLE OF MAXIMUMS

Several years ago, I was getting ready to build a pole barn on my property. I was talking about it with a cousin of mine and decided to ask him how big of a barn he thought was big enough. He said, "Just a little bit bigger." We both laughed, but I think most of us live by that philosophy. When it comes to how much is enough, it always is a little bit more.

I think most people can relate, which is why this concept of maximums is so important. But in case there is any confusion about what living by maximums is all about, this chapter will hopefully resolve it.

Living your financial life by setting maximums is about having a vision for how much is enough and living that vision out. It is about knowing what we need and not being taken in by greed, both of which take discipline. Just to be clear, maximums is not minimalism. Minimalists live with the fewest number of things possible and seem to take pride in how little they have. While this certainly can free up resources to increase generosity, generosity isn't always the goal of minimalism. But it is for maximums. In fact, the very goal of living a life of maximums is always to free up resources in order to be more generous. Several top experts have introduced the concept of maximums in their works:

> A Christian should have a goal of how much he wants to accumulate—maximum, not minimum. Think in terms of storing for provision rather than storing for protection.
> —Larry Burkett. *Your Finances in Changing Times* [1]

What if we put simple caps on our lifestyles and
were free to give the rest of our resources away?

—David Platt, *Radical: Taking Back Your Faith
from the American Dream*[2]

Second, establish a reasonable standard of living.
We need to develop our lifestyle based upon our
convictions, not our circumstances.

—Jill and Mark Savage, *Living with Less
So Your Family Has More*[3]

We require another vision of life, a vision in which the word
"enough" plays a positive role. The implementation of such
a vision will create new possibilities for *neighborliness*, for
demonstrating *care for our surroundings*, and for having more
time available in our harried lives. Such a vision will help to
liberate not only the poor but also the *rich*.

—Goudzwaard, Lange, and Vennen, *Beyond Poverty
and Affluence: Toward an Economy of Care with a
Twelve-Step Program for Economic Recovery*[4]

Larry Burkett once said he counseled people of all different income
levels, each who were struggling to live on what they made. He said
that if you took the $200,000 a year one family was making and gave
that income to the family making $25,000 a year, the family mak-
ing $25,000 would be rich beyond their wildest imagination. If that
was the case, why did the family making $200,000 struggle to have
enough? It wasn't an issue of income; it was an issue of spending and
desire. For most of us, desire is the real issue. When we can control
our desire, we have enough. When we can be like Paul, who states
in Philippians 4 that he has *learned* to be content, we have enough.
How do we do this? Paul says he learned to do this through God who
gives us strength. With God, we can learn to be content, too.

In a short article called "Minimalist Living: When a Lot Less Is
More," Josh Sanburn shows how study after study indicates that possessions don't bring happiness. He discusses a minimalist lifestyle and

tries to show how having more doesn't make us any happier.[5] Witherington also states, "Despite the numerous scriptural warnings about the deleterious effects of wealth and prosperity on one's spiritual life, we still continue to strive for material success, go to motivational seminars, and live lives of conspicuous consumption."[6] Sider gives a solution and a warning, "God's people must practice self-denial to aid the poor and share the gospel. But we must maintain a biblical balance. It is not because food, clothes, wealth, and property are inherently evil that Christians today must lower their standard of living. It is because others are starving."[7]

I often tell my students that I hope they become extremely wealthy. Not so they can have a lot of stuff, but so they can give a lot away and impact the world for Christ. I don't believe wealth is wrong. But keeping wealth for ourselves while others are in need is wrong. Jesus teaches this as well. When the rich man fails to help Lazarus, the poor man who is right outside his gate, the rich man goes to hell (Luke 16). That should teach us something.

I believe there will be some people who have been so gifted in making money that they won't be able to give money away fast enough. They will become extremely wealthy. But that shouldn't automatically mean they should live a "rich" lifestyle. They just won't be able to give it all away fast enough. But for most of us, this won't be the case, and that's totally fine. When we want to be like the people who can't help but make a lot of money, we fall into a trap and begin worshipping mammon—money—instead of God.

Randy Alcorn, in his book *The Treasure Principle* says, "We take care of our needs and why shouldn't the rest go toward treasure in heaven?"[8] This is a new mindset for many of us, the practice of which frees us to be what God has created us to be. I am a college professor. I believe this is what God has called me to be, at least for now. At one point in my career, I left education to take a CFO position at a large, non-profit childcare organization. To this day I believe taking that position was God's will and I was obedient in leaving education for a time. But God clearly showed me He wanted me back in education, and I took a pay cut to go back. It was the second pay cut I had taken to teach college. The first time it was about a 70 percent pay cut!

At one time, I was the corporate controller for the largest privately-owned long-term care company in Indiana. After being in that role for about four years, my spirit grew restless. I have learned this is often how God prompts us for change. I thought I was supposed to change jobs within the corporate world and so began a "quiet" job search. After about a year with a lot of interviews but no job offers, my wife told me God wanted me to immediately finish the MBA I was pursuing. I still had four classes left, which would have required leaving my full-time position and being a full-time student with no income and four children to support. So I told my wife that this was a crazy idea. My wife, as is her wise custom, told me to pray about it.

As I prayed, I became convinced she was correct. God wanted me to finish my MBA as soon as possible. I had pursued the MBA because I was sure God was calling me to teach at the college level someday, but I believed it would be several years into the future. I asked for a meeting with my boss at work so I could discuss this with him. I still wanted to work part-time, if possible, to have some income while I finished the MBA and to keep the door open for me to continue the same job after I finished the MBA. When I met with my boss, he told me the company I was working for was hoping to promote me to chief financial officer. That was a surprise. I was thirty-four years old and being the CFO of such a large organization at that young of an age was beyond anything I had dreamed. I was torn.

But my wife and I were both convinced God wanted me to finish the MBA, and I came to agreement with the company to work part-time and take classes full-time for a semester. About a week after we came to this agreement, Grace College called me and asked if I would teach one class for them. I turned that opportunity down because of my recent agreement with the company where I worked but told them I truly believed God was calling me to teach college full-time someday. The person I was talking with said, "That's interesting. We have a full-time position in accounting open. Why don't you apply?" I did apply and started teaching full-time in January after finishing the MBA in December. It was about two years later when Rebecca, our fifth child, was born with major health issues, causing her to spend most of her life at Riley Hospital for Children at IU Health in Indianapolis. Our lives were crazy as we tried to care for Rebecca's needs and the needs of our four other children. I believe the only way we survived that time was because God knew our family needed the flexible schedule teaching college provided during the time our daughter spent in the hospital. God always provided enough for us to live on. Not nearly as much as we had before, but enough.

Two years after Rebecca died, I left my teaching position to become CFO of the child-care organization. After I left the CFO position and went back to education, the organization I left came to me and offered to double my salary if I would return. I didn't think twice. I said no. I knew that a big pay increase would not mean changing my standard of living. It would mean I could give more money away, but it also would mean I would be leaving a job I totally believed God called me to do at this time in my life. I would be chasing money and not following God. Therefore, saying no was easy.

That wasn't the first time I had said no to money. The first time I said no would have made me a multi-millionaire. The company I was working for was starting a management company, and the six majority owners asked me to be a minority owner. I was excited about the opportunity. My wife was not, however. As we processed the opportunity, I became convinced God was saying this was not for us. While I didn't know I would have become wealthy at the time of the offer, I had a pretty good idea it could happen—a $25,000 investment would have turned into several million in wages and dividends over a seven-year span. I was corporate controller for the company, so I knew everyone's wages and dividends. But saying yes at that time probably would have kept me from ever becoming a professor and would have changed the direction of my life. I probably would not have pursued an MBA, would not have been academically qualified to teach college, and would never have taken the teaching position at Grace College. One decision can change the trajectory of your life, and I wouldn't change the way mine has gone for anything.

Paul uses accounting terminology in Philippians 4:17 when he says God has an account he credits for each of us when we are generous. If we understand this correctly, that means whatever we give we will get back some day. Living by maximums not only frees us from greed today, it adds to the account God has for us later. In other words, living by maximums has both current reward and future reward. We gain today, and we gain later. I'm very glad I said no to those other opportunities. I truly believe by saying no and being obedient to God's call on my life, I have been able to add to my account in heaven. Plus, I'm right where I belong.

There is another area related to money where God asks us to be obedient—tithing. In fact, a major factor in living by maximums is to help us become obedient in this area. In the next chapter, I will explain the tithe from a New Testament perspective and show how tithing could become a powerful influence in our world for Christ.

THINK AND DISCUSS

1. Have you ever set a maximum for your own financial life? What was it?

   _____

   _____

   _____

2. Do you believe possessions bring lasting happiness? How have you experienced happiness or lack of happiness from possessions?

   _____

   _____

   _____

LIVING IT OUT

1. Set a maximum related to your financial life. Write it down. Show it to someone you trust.

2. Go to your bank and set up a separate contribution or giving account. Arrange to have money direct deposited into the account or have an automatic transfer set up to move money into the account each month.

4.
THE RELATIONSHIP BETWEEN TITHING AND MAXIMUMS

My preteen years were spent in a square, almost plantation-style house with four large, white pillars reaching to the top of the second story of the house. The back of the house had a room that stretched the entire width of the house made almost entirely of huge windows on the outside wall. A limestone fireplace stretched nearly half the length of the inside wall of the room.

It must have been shortly after my tenth birthday and I had been given the most money I had ever seen in my life—ten dollars! I remember sitting on the hearth of that large fireplace with my mother as she explained to me what the Bible taught about money. I should give a tithe, 10 percent, from the gift I had received. I was devastated. Back then, candy bars cost five cents and my birthday money represented about two hundred candy bars. I was rich! Giving up the potential for twenty candy bars seemed extreme to me.

I don't remember all my mom said but I do remember that she did not force me to give a dollar, but I gave the money, probably in the Sunday School offering at church. To this day, I believe it was a decisive moment in my life. Was I going to honor God by recognizing that all I have or can have comes from Him? Or would I keep all I could for myself? I'm sure glad I gave that dollar.

Tithing is one of the topics Christians just don't want to talk about, but understanding the tithe is critically important to understanding the heart of God and money. There are several different opinions on the topic. I believe practicing the tithe in this New Testament era is still valid, sort of, which I will explain later. It seems pretty certain that Jesus validates the tithe in his conversation with the Pharisees as recorded in Matthew 23:23–28. Jesus states that the Pharisees should

33

continue to tithe on even the smallest income but calls out other ways they are falling short. Some people believe Jesus' statement in this passage was meant for the Pharisees and not for Christians. But I find nothing in any New Testament scriptures which would suggest the practice of tithing ceased with the coming of Jesus.

The tithe has its beginnings when Abram rescued his nephew, Lot, from captivity. Abram takes back what had been stolen and gives a tenth of it to Melchizedek, king of Salem and "priest of God Most High" (Gen. 14:16–20). It was after this event in the Old Testament that we see the practice of the tithe, which seems to serve a couple of purposes: 1) it provides for the priests or what we would equate to those who serve in full-time ministry, and 2) it recognizes dependence on God. When we look at Malachi, the last book of the Old Testament, God says that not giving a full tithe equates to robbing Him. In fact, it brings a curse upon them. The full tithe mentioned was probably much more than 10 percent. It seems to have included their equivalent of taxes today. In total it might have been closer to 30 percent. This amount was used for maintaining both the priestly functions and the government.

Some have suggested since we pay taxes to our government today, we are somehow not required to tithe. Most people in the United States pay 20 percent or less of their income to the government. This amount is made up of 7.65 percent of FICA taxes (Social Security and Medicare), state and local income taxes of around 5 percent, and an effective federal income tax rate of between 3 and 10 percent. A family of four making $100,000 a year will pay an effective rate of about 8 to 9 percent in federal income tax. A family of four making $50,000 a year will pay an effective rate of about 3 to 4 percent in federal income tax (depending on allowed deductions for health insurance and so forth). So it takes an income of around $100,000 per year for a family to reach the 20 percent effective tax rate (7.65 + 5 + 8 = 20.65) and this includes something we are supposed to get back in retirement—Social Security. In 2016, the median household income was around $60,000, so most households are not hitting the 20 percent effective tax rate.

Studies of giving in the United States consistently show Christians donate somewhere around 3 percent of their gross income to church and other charitable interests combined. By any measure, this falls far short of a tithe. A 2008 Barna Group study suggests that only 9 percent of "born again" adults contribute 10 percent or more of their income. Evangelicals are the most generous with 24 percent contributing at least 10 percent of their income.[1] A 2013 Barna Group study reports that 12 percent of "born again" adults were tithing.[2] Another Barna Group study in 2017 seems to confirm these percentages with about 12.5 percent (25 percent of the 50 percent of all Christians who are classified by Barna as "givers") of all Christians planning to give 10 percent or more of their income to charity.[3]

Based on these survey results, it is obvious the church in the United States doesn't sufficiently practice tithing today. Ron Sider in his book *Rich Christians in an Age of Hunger* states that in 1960, one-fifth of the world's people living in the richest nations enjoyed an income thirty times more than those living in the poorest one-fifth.[4] This number grew to fifty times by 2005.[5] We are getting relatively richer than poorer people in the world but we aren't giving more. "In 2011, the wealthiest Americans (top 20 percent in earnings) gave 1.3 percent of their income to charity. The bottom 20 percent gave 3.2 percent."[6] It seems making more money does not increase the percentage we give to charity.

Earlier in this section, I said I believe the tithe is still valid, "sort of." Let me explain. When we look at the teachings of Jesus, we often find Him taking an Old Testament concept and explaining what God intended. In Matthew 6, Jesus makes a few "when you" statements. One of those is "when you give to the needy" (v. 2). Jesus doesn't say, "if you give to the needy." He assumes people gave. In this particular passage, the message seems to be that we don't make a big deal out of giving. It should just be something we do without needing to be praised by others or commanded to do. It should come naturally.

In the New Testament, Jesus never seemed to decrease the requirements of the law, He always increases the requirements. He expands on them, like it isn't just the act of adultery that was wrong, it is wrong just to *contemplate* adultery. It isn't just wrong to kill someone, hating them is also wrong. Most Christians would agree that it is our attitudes that lead to action, and God is concerned with both our attitudes *and* our actions. How would it be any different with tithing? If giving 10 percent was the Old Testament minimum, why would it decrease or become irrelevant in the New Testament? Wouldn't it be tested by both our attitude and our actions? Would one of the richest societies to ever live on this earth be asked to only give 10 percent? That hardly seems like something Jesus would have taught.

In Luke 12, Jesus tells a story about stewardship. Jesus says that the wise manager adequately provides for those under his care. But if the manager believes the master (owner) will not be back soon and begins to mishandle the master's interests, there will be severe consequences (vv. 42–46). Jesus goes on to say that if we know what the master wants and fail to carry out the master's wishes, we will be severely punished (v. 47). If we have been given much, much is expected of us, and if we have "been entrusted with much, much more will be asked" (v. 48). I don't believe there is any doubt that Christians living in the United States today have been entrusted with much when compared to most of the rest of the world. We have also been entrusted with much when compared to almost every historical generation. I have no doubt that God is asking much more of us.

Let's put some numbers to giving. There are approximately 325 million people living in the United States. If only 15 percent are devoted Christians (and this number is probably pretty close) and a family is assumed to be five people, there are about fifty million people living in devoted Christian families and about ten million families (325 million x 15 percent divided by 5). If the average family income is only $50,000 a year for these families (and it probably is somewhat higher than this) and each family gave only 1 percent more of their income per year, this would equate to $5 billion more giving per year by just Christian families. Every extra 1 percent in giving by Christian families equals close to $5 billion extra per year to maintain churches, help the poor, and reach the world with the gospel. If the church in just the United States gave 10 percent instead of 3 percent, that would be an extra $35 billion per year. Sider puts this number at $46 billion per year.[7] How long would it take to reach the whole world with the gospel if we would just tithe? Probably not very long.

I believe the tithe is still valid but, for most of us, we should be giving quite a bit more than 10 percent of our income. In our society, we struggle with serving money rather than it serving us. "Serving money is often difficult to identify because loving money is a respectable sin—people will congratulate you for acquiring the trappings of financial success."[8] We all like to be praised by people, so we do things that bring us praise, such as buying nicer stuff. Lynn Miller in his book *The Power of Enough* states, "When things take on the wrong meaning, then you have a problem. And it's a spiritual problem."[9] In Philippians 4, Paul talks about how he has learned to be content no matter what his financial circumstances. He then makes a powerful statement which is often misquoted. In verse 13, Paul states that he can be content "through him who gives me strength." Paul says it is God's strength that has allowed him to learn how to be content. When was the last time we asked God to give us strength to be content? Instead, we try to find contentment by getting more stuff. I think most of us have found that having more stuff does not bring contentment.

That doesn't mean tithing or giving much more than the tithe is easy, even if we become better and better stewards of what God has allowed us to have. "The call to discipleship is a call to stewardship. It is not meant to be easy, nor is it always filled with pleasure. In fact, it is often difficult and incessantly demanding."[10]

If you are reading this and just don't believe you can afford to tithe, you are probably being hindered by fear. In Malachi 3:8–9, the prophet makes a pretty clear statement that not offering God the tithe equates to robbing Him and that the people are under a curse for not bringing the full tithe. Then God makes an interesting statement through the prophet Malachi. God says that when we tithe, He provides for us generously and prevents bad things from happening (vv. 10–11). Verse 10 is the only time I am aware of in the Bible where God tells His people to test Him and see if He won't do what He promises.

When we believe we don't have enough to tithe, we are not trusting God. I know of two families from the church I attended in my twenties and thirties who were struggling financially. When they decided to trust that God would provide for their needs if they began tithing, they testified to how they seemed to have more money after giving 10 percent away than they had when they kept 100 percent of what they earned. In our own logic, this just doesn't make sense. But I believe God is true to His word, and somehow, He can make 90 percent go further than 100 percent. If you are not yet practicing tithing, I challenge you to test God by beginning to tithe and see what He does. See if He doesn't just throw open the storehouses of heaven on you (Mal. 3:10).

THINK AND DISCUSS

1. What have you learned in this chapter about the tithe that you didn't know before?

   _____

   _____

   _____

2. Do you believe what God said through the prophet Malachi? Why or why not?

   _____

   _____

   _____

LIVING IT OUT

1. If you currently don't give a full tithe of your income, begin giving. If you don't believe you can give a full 10 percent now, start giving some anyway with a defined timeline of when you will be giving 10 percent. Pray that God will help you to trust Him in this.

2. Have someone you trust hold you accountable to complete step 1 above.

5.
HOW MAXIMUMS RELATE TO OUR STANDARD OF LIVING: FOOD, CLOTHES, SHOES

"We can find solace in the fact that Paul 'learned'
contentment. It did not come to him naturally."
—Dave Sutherland and Kirk Nowery[1]

Setting maximums on your basic standard of living will mean one thing—learning to be content with what you have been given. If contentment is learned, I'm sure it will probably take some time to master. I often encourage my college students to make the decision while they are in college to set maximums on the lifestyle they will maintain after college. I can't tell them what their own maximums should be, and this isn't just an academic exercise—it is life-changing. I have had previous students who talked with me about how they took my encouragement seriously and are now setting maximums for their financial lives. They made this adjustment early in life and I'm sure maintaining a lifestyle with less than they could have early on will likely be easier for them than for those of us who decide to set maximums later in life. But it can still be done, though for us it might be much more of a painful process.

It is sort of like dieting. When you decide you want to lose weight, you know you have to change something. I have found the fastest thing to change is to just eat less. But eating less is hard. At first your stomach is larger than it needs to be and you feel hungry when you don't eat as much as you used to. You have to go to bed hungry and that is uncomfortable. The first couple of nights are really hard and you might not sleep very well. But after a few nights of denying yourself the food your body craves, your stomach shrinks and you don't feel hungry at night anymore. I have lost fifteen pounds, or close to 9 percent of my overall weight, in about twelve weeks, and I wasn't much overweight to begin with. All I did was eat less.

Starting off with maximums is a lot like this. You just need to *buy* less. It will be really hard at first and you might fail a few times. But over time, you can train yourself to not buy things you don't really need and it will become easier. You will learn to be content with what you already have and will free up money to give. Just like being on a diet, you must learn to not pay attention to how much other people are eating but only eat what you need. Howard Dayton says in *Your Money Counts*, "We are not born with the instinct for contentment; rather, it is learned."[2] We have to learn what we need and what we really don't need. That doesn't mean we are so legalistic on spending money that we never buy anything we just want. But we know when we are buying things we just want and have set limits on such spending. Budgeting helps, but budgeting is only as good as our self-control.

I said in an earlier chapter that I don't believe a life of asceticism is necessary. This is a lifestyle spent depriving oneself of all but the bare necessities. I don't see much in the way of biblical evidence to support such an extreme lifestyle.[3] Sutherland and Nowery put it this way, "It's easy in a culture of abundance to define 'essentials' in a much broader sense than God ever intended. We should in fact think as simply as possible, being willing to be satisfied with food to eat, clothes to wear, and a place to live."[4] Somewhere in between what they said and asceticism is probably where most of us will choose to live. But I do believe we need to define "essentials" and then decide whether we will be satisfied with that or something a little more. Deciding we need a lot more than what is essential will leave little left to give. The trick is to find the balance. Andy Stanley says, "We possess more than most people around the world and throughout history could ever dream about. We have everything we need. But we lose sight of what we need it for."[5] This is so true and I think this is a good question to ask as we determine our maximums. We should ask ourselves questions like, "What do I need this for?" If it is to sustain life, it really is a need. If it is just to make us feel good, it is a luxury.

That doesn't mean we don't ever buy things we don't really need, but we have set a maximum on that type of purchase.

Lynn Miller's book *The Power of Enough* is a good reminder that we all have the power to say we have enough. It boils down to being content with some standard of living we have defined for ourselves. When we say we have enough, the tactics of marketers won't have their intended effect.[6] But we all have to decide what is enough for us. Jeff Shinaberg explains "enough" in this way:

> The definition of *enough* cannot be defined by or for others. It would be much easier if someone gave each of us a definition to live by, but it isn't that easy. *Enough* isn't a percentage of your income. There is no simple formula. Every person must define what is enough individually.[7]

This book isn't just meant to be a theoretical discussion of maximums but is intended to give some practical advice about how to start deciding what is enough for you. This will apply to all of what makes up our standard of living, from food to clothing, where we live, what car we drive, and our other possessions. I will talk about all of these in this and future chapters, but since food is so critical to us, let's start there.

Food and Beverages

"The dollar value of the food Americans throw away each year is more than one-quarter of the total annual income of all the Christians in Africa."[8]

Growing up, I remember my parents making comments about eating all the food on my plate. I generally didn't have a problem with eating all my food when I was younger; I just ate too much and was rather chubby. Unfortunately, that mindset has carried over to my adult life and I tend to eat all I have in front of me even when I don't need that much. The problem isn't really eating all the food on my plate; it is putting too much food on my plate. Taking only the amount of food we really need is a process. When we eat quickly, we don't feel full and tend to overeat. If we spend time eating more slowly, we begin to feel full and won't eat as much.

There is also a psychological part to eating that begins with the size of our plate. We tend to fill our plate no matter what size of plate we have. If we start with a smaller plate, we will take less food. Try it sometime. It really works. Maybe the first way to limit spending money on food is to spend some money on smaller plates!

You would be surprised at how much money is spent on eating out. If you work outside the home and eat lunch out most days, you are probably spending close to $2,000 a year eating out even if you only eat out about 200 days a year. Most of us work about forty-eight weeks a year (considering vacation time) so 200 days eating out is a reasonable number. If we eat out for lunch 200 times, at about ten dollars per day it is $2,000. But if you would pack your lunch about half those days, you could generate close to $1,000 a year to give away. If you did this for all your work career, you would give close to $40,000 more away in your lifetime in today's dollars. With inflation, it adds up to a lot more. If you are married and both spouses make this decision, your family could probably generate about $100,000 over your work life to give away from just choosing to not eat out at lunch as often. This is the power of setting maximums. When you practice this discipline over a lifetime, the amount of money generated to give away and increase the credit in your heavenly account is truly amazing.

I realize there is a lot of variation in how often families eat out for dinner, so I'll just use one example. If you eat out twice a week and cut back to once a week, a family of four could generate (after food and tip) approximately fifty dollars more per week. Kids grow up and leave the home so there is a two-part process to determine the savings. Let's say you have ten years of four people eating out and forty years of two people eating out. For ten years, your food savings for eating out once per week instead of twice per week is roughly $50 per week or $2,500 per year (fifty weeks eating out per year). Ten years of saving $2,500 is $25,000. The other forty years would mean saving half as much per year or $1,250 per year times forty years equals $50,000. Over the fifty years of not eating out as much, the savings is close to $75,000. I realize you will need to pay for food you eat at home when not eating out, but that cost should be about 30 percent of the cost of eating out (or less), so the net savings would still be close to $52,500 without considering inflation.

If you currently buy lunch every day, eat out twice a week at night, and are willing to cut that in half, you could generate close to $150,000 over your lifetime to give away. Based on most Christians giving about 3 percent of their income away per year, $150,000 is more than a lifetime of giving. If we assume the average Christian family makes $50,000 per year and gives 3 percent or $1,500 per year over forty-five years of working, that family would give a total of $67,500 or a little less than half of what might be generated from just eating out less. Eating out less and giving the saved amount away could double the giving of many Christians!

There is also the issue of spending more on food we eat at home. A 2013 article by *USA Today* reported a moderate-cost plan for feeding a family of four to be $239 per week.[9] Rounded off, this equals about $1,000 per month or $12,000 per year. If you don't know how much you are spending on food, you need to begin tracking this cost. Our family has experienced some food allergies over the past several years, which means buying some more expensive grains. But we have never spent more than $10,000 per year in food and that was feeding a family of six or seven people. So, I know the amount spent on food can be less than $12,000 per year. If you can save $2,000 per year on food you prepare at home, you can generate $100,000 over fifty years. This may mean buying more generic food and less prepared food. It will depend on where you set your maximums for food.

If we now combine the savings from eating out less frequently and the savings from being more frugal in the food consumed at home, the savings from food alone is around $250,000 in a lifetime ($150,000 from eating out less plus $100,000 for spending less at home).

Specialty drinks could be another way to generate money to give. If you get a specialty coffee or other drink each day and spend $2.50 on it, you spend about $900 per year on these drinks ($2.50 x 360 days). Over forty years, this equals $36,000 spent on those drinks. A couple of dollars doesn't sound like much a day, but it really adds up over a lifetime. Having a specialty drink only two days a week and either going without or drinking something less expensive the other days would generate a lot of money to give.

On a practical note before going on to the other categories, it might be helpful to know how to save the money you don't spend on food and drink. I have found it helpful to not ever have access to money I am saving by spending less. Twice a month, automatic transfers occur where my bank has been told to transfer a set amount of money out of my general savings account to other accounts, including my contribution account. Once you have decided to spend less on food and drink, have that savings automatically taken out of the account(s) you use to spend on living expenses and have the money put into your contribution account. This assures you don't use the savings from food to just buy other things you want.

Clothing and Shoes

Therefore I tell you, do not worry about your
life, what you will eat or drink; or about your
body, what you will wear. Is not life more than food,
and the body more than clothes?
—Matthew 6:25

Your beauty should not come from outward adornment,
such as elaborate hairstyles and the wearing of gold
jewelry or fine clothes. Rather, it should be that of your
inner self, the unfading beauty of a gentle and quiet
spirit, which is of great worth in God's sight.
—1 Peter 3:3, 4

In Matthew, Jesus is recorded as saying not to worry about food and clothes. I think Jesus put these two together because they are things we all need. We all need something to eat and things to wear. Without anything to wear, we would die in extreme climates (at worst) or be immodest (at best). Neither would be acceptable. So we must have things to wear. In the 1 Peter passage above, "Paul then is not merely arguing here for modest apparel, but against ostentatious, flashy, and distracting apparel. Such apparel goes against the rules of modesty, discretion, propriety, and sobriety that were to apply to everyone in worship, especially when meeting in close quarters."[10]

When it comes to modesty, I believe clothing should be modest for both women and men. We all have different views on what clothing is deemed modest, so I won't even try to address that issue. What I will address, though, is how much we could save by not spending as much on clothing. For most people, the savings available on clothing are not as dramatic as the savings available on food. A lot of the issue with clothing is whether you are buying clothes when you need them or just because you have become tired of what you currently own. Most of us probably don't own any, or much, gaudy clothing. So, we tend to read what Peter wrote and dismiss it. But we do often own a lot of clothing, much of which sits in the back of our closets for years. I find it interesting that John the Baptist, when asked what should be done to please God, mentions giving extra things we have to the needy. If John really was speaking God's heart, and most of us would agree he was, then he is saying that we should not be keeping more than we need. I was helping an elderly couple move once and was astounded at the amount of clothing they owned. It had to be at least ten times as many articles of clothing as I own. Don't get me wrong; I have clothes I don't wear very often and probably some clothes I don't wear at all. I did a purge about a year ago but still have some things I don't really wear. I'm sure you can relate.

Carl Kreider, in his book *The Christian Entrepreneur*, does a good job of addressing clothing. He suggests buying a few, high-quality sets of clothes that will not go out of style and wear them for a long time.[11] You might spend a little more per set but you will not be spending as much on clothes per year. Overall, you will actually spend less. "The great tempter of our time is Walmart."[12] Walmart doesn't sell high-end clothing; they sell inexpensive, cheaply-made stuff. This seems like it would be a good idea to purchase inexpensive clothes from there, but if we aren't careful, we can spend a lot of money buying clothes that wear out quickly. When I asked the couple I helped move about all their clothes, they said two things: 1) they had just given a lot of their clothes away before the move, and

2) most of what they had bought was from second-hand stores. Well, I was really glad they had given some of it away before the move because we still moved an awful lot of clothes. On one hand, I'm glad they hadn't spent as much on clothes as they would have spent by buying all those clothes brand new. On the other hand, they still didn't come close to living the way John the Baptist said. They still had way too many clothes; I think they could have worn a different piece each day over the entire year. Most of us don't have that many clothes.

The average amount spent on clothing per year is somewhere between 3 to 5 percent of our income.[13] If we make $50,000 per year and spend an average amount on clothes, we spend between $1,500 and $2,500 per year, which is between about $125 to $200 per month. Over our working life of about forty-five years, that would be $67,500 to $108,000 on clothes. Sure, some clothes wear out each year and might need to be replaced. And our bodies do change over the years so we have to buy some new, better-fitting clothes. But not getting caught up on spending on clothes when we really don't need anything could generate some pretty large savings over our lifetimes. If we spent half as much on clothes as the average, we could generate between $33,750 ($67,500/2) to $54,000 ($108,000/2) to give away.

How about shoes? There seems to be a stereotype that women continually buy shoes. Research on the topic shows that an average American woman will spend around $20,000 on shoes in her lifetime. So, it isn't even close to the amount spent on clothes, but it is still a pretty big number. The average woman owns about 17 pairs of shoes, while the average man owns about 11 pairs.[14] I own right at 11 pairs of all types of shoes and boots. This includes my snow boots, work shoes, running shoes, bicycling shoes, dress shoes, and so forth. I think the total amount I have spent on all of these is about $500. I have had some of them for twenty-plus years and they are still in good shape. I don't think I'll hit the $20,000 amount in my lifetime but will probably be closer to $2,000. I think Kreider's general principle works for shoes, too. Buy good quality shoes that will last a long time and wear them out. Don't get caught up in changing fashions—

this is what gets us in trouble. I realize this is probably easier for men than women as fashions change so rapidly for women and they have the added pressure to have shoes that match the fashion.

I think Paul's encouragement to not get caught up in fancy dress applies pretty well to us today. You get to choose. Will you get caught up in fashion or not? Will you choose to forfeit future heavenly credit for more clothes and shoes to wear around today? That is what you are actually choosing. My encouragement to you is to learn to be content with the clothes and shoes you have. When you need them, think about the quality of what you are buying and whether spending a little more would get you something that will last longer, making it cheaper overall. While you might want to budget some money monthly for these items, don't spend it unless you really need something.

Again, saving money in this area doesn't mean you go out and buy more clothes or shoes or spend the savings on recreation and other stuff you want—it means you can have more to give away.

That is the goal.

That is the purpose we are after.

Food and clothes are two categories where most of us could generate savings to give more money away. In the following chapters, we will explore other lifestyle categories where setting maximums can increase generosity. The next chapter we will explore how we can set maximums on housing and debt.

THINK AND DISCUSS

1. In which areas of life do you struggle to be content?

_____

_____

_____

2. Have you ever given clothes or shoes away without buying more? If so, how did that make you feel?

_____

_____

_____

LIVING IT OUT

1. If you don't have a way to track your spending each month, begin one. It can be as simple as tracking your spending for various categories (food, clothes, and so forth) on a piece of paper. Most banks have an online method of tracking spending. Choose a category of spending you know you can spend less in and have the amount you will now save moved into your contribution account.

2. Give something away that you don't use and don't need.

6.
HOUSING
AND DEBT

A few months after our fifth child Rebecca was born, we sold our house so we could move closer to Grace College where I worked. But we had to be out of one house before we could move into the next house, and it took four months before we moved in. During those four months, we moved three times and lived in two other houses that were about one-half the size of the house we had sold. I don't remember living in much smaller houses being a bad experience, partly because we weren't focused on our housing situation. We were more focused on our daughter, who had severe medical issues and required a lot of our time and energy. For the most part, we were content with our housing.

In this chapter, I want to keep the real purpose of housing in perspective as a guide for how much to spend on housing expenses. What do we need housing for? How many people need to be housed? Is location an issue? What is realistic given the earning situation? Andy Stanley raises an interesting point, "We possess more than most people around the world and throughout history could ever dream about. We have everything we need. But we lose sight of what we need it for."[1] It is important to consider the basics sometimes.

Consider this: in 2015, the average size of a new house was 2,687 square feet. In 1973, the average was 1,660 square feet.[2] In 42 years, the average size of a house increased by about 62 percent, while the average family size has decreased. A check on Zillow.com shows the average square feet of houses selling near where I live at a little over

1,500 square feet. Of course, this reflects houses selling that were built in the 1970s and before. The average family size based on the 2010 U.S. government census is 2.6 people so that means the average new house is over 1,000 square feet per person. Our house is pretty close to the new average. Much of the time we have owned this house we have had eight people living there. That equates to less than 400 square feet per person. Most of the time, we have plenty of space. When all of our children and their spouses show up, we have twelve people in the house, and they often stay overnight. It can be a little tight, but we manage.

So, what has happened over the past 40 years? Some would speculate we entertain more and need the space when we have people over. My experience would say otherwise. When I was young, we almost always had people over for lunch on Sunday or we went to someone's house for lunch. It was what we did. The size of the house didn't matter. Today, I don't find the same degree of entertaining for most people. How about you?

Also, families don't have as many children, on average, today as they had 40 years ago, but something else related to children has definitely changed. Most children today have their own bedrooms and tend to spend more time in their rooms than I remember spending in mine. Forty years ago, most children shared bedrooms with their siblings. We slept in our bedroom and I don't remember spending much other time in it. Today children have computers, electronic games, televisions, and often other "toys" in their bedroom, so they spend a lot more time there. Maybe eliminating some of those items from bedrooms would mean less time spent there and bedrooms could again be shared more easily. Oftentimes today, the first time a teenager has had to share a bedroom is when he or she gets to college. It can be a traumatic experience. Plus when they are holed up in their bedroom all the time, there is less time spent developing social skills or building community with others. I believe God created us for community, and the first place to learn the skills necessary for that to happen is in the family.

Let's face it; you just can't hide as easily in a smaller house. Having larger houses and larger living spaces allow us to get away from society and hide in our houses. I grew up in the country and we spent a lot of time outside working and playing, which allowed us to get to know our neighbors. I know of people who have lived years in the same house and eventually moved, having never even known the names of their neighbors. Larger houses allow us to hide away from community. That doesn't mean that everyone who lives in a large home does not communicate with their neighbors. I am suggesting large homes allow us to hide away more easily and may lead to less involvement with our neighborhood and community than what took place forty years ago.

Other aspects of housing have changed over the last 40 years, too: master suites are huge, there are more bathrooms than people to use them, larger living spaces, and so on, all of which comes with a much larger price tag. The median house price for November 2017 was about $248,000. This is not building a new house but buying a used one. A Zillow search of where I live shows a median selling price of about $180,000. Of course, the selling price depends greatly on where you live. One of my doctoral cohort friends just took a new job in another state, bought a used house which was of similar size to the house he sold, and paid around 60 percent more for the new house. His property taxes are going to be about three times what he was paying. Where you live really does change the cost of housing.

More expensive housing also means bigger mortgages. I agree with Blomberg that there are only two reasons to borrow money: housing and education.[3] While borrowing money for other things might need to happen when you are young and first starting a career (such as a car), you should quickly work your way to paying cash for all purchases other than a house and education. For most of us, being able to save enough to pay cash for a house is not very feasible. I know a couple who did this when they were young and before they had any children. They lived in a very cheap basement apartment for a few years, both worked professional jobs, saved everything they made above their living expenses, and paid cash for a modest house. It can be done but you must have a lot of self-control and a job that pays pretty well.

Most of us will need to save a down payment and buy a modest house. When interest rates are relatively low like they have been since the 2008 recession, buying a house often uses less cash flow than renting even when you pay insurance and property taxes. This depends on the part of the United States where you live. Let's put some numbers to the cost of housing.

If you save a 20 percent down payment and buy a modestly-priced, $125,000 house, you need to borrow $100,000. Table 1 below shows how much it costs over the life of the loan for buying this house. If you have been paying rent and saving money for the down payment, you should be able to afford paying extra per month to pay off the loan earlier and thus saving some interest over the life of the loan. You can save about $100,000 overall if you pay off the loan in ten years instead of thirty years. You could give away the money you saved to increase your heavenly credit.

Table 1
Total Paid on House Loan

		30 year	20 year	15 year	10 year
Principal	$100,000	$100,000	$100,000	$100,000	$100,000
Rate	5.00%	5.00%	5.00%	5.00%	5.00%
Years		30	20	15	10
Payment		$537	$660	$791	$1,061
Insurance	1%	$83	$83	$83	$83
Property Taxes	1%	$83	$83	$83	$83
Total payment		$703	$827	$957	$1,227
Total paid over life of loan:		$253,256	$198,389	$172,343	$147,279

Most people pay on their mortgage for a few years, build up some equity in their first house, and then make some upgrades. There are some good reasons to upgrade, such as when God blesses you with more children than you expected. But often we upgrade only because we want something bigger and nicer, not because we need something bigger and nicer. I believe social media and general connectedness to information has a lot to do with our perceived need for a larger and nicer/newer house. We are able to see what other people own and that creates desire within us for something similar. So, whether we really need a bigger house or not, we decide to buy a bigger house. Table 2 gives an example for what happens when you choose to do this. If when you have owned your first house for several years and even just paid the minimum mortgage payment, you might be able to buy a $200,000 house and borrow $150,000 because you have built up $50,000 equity on your first house. I'm not suggesting you should do this, just giving an example.

Table 2
Total Paid on House Loan for Upgraded House (example)

		30 year	20 year	15 year	10 year
Principal	**$150,000**	$150,000	$150,000	$150,000	$150,000
Rate	**5.00%**	5.00%	5.00%	5.00%	5.00%
Years		30	20	15	10
Payment		$805	$990	$1,186	$1,591
Insurance	**1%**	$125	$125	$125	$125
Property Taxes	**1%**	$125	$125	$125	$125
Total payment		$1,055	$1,240	$1,436	$1,841
Total paid over life of loan:		**$379,884**	**$297,584**	**$258,514**	**$220,918**

I think the major issue for most people when it comes to housing is contentment, or rather a lack of it. When we allow our focus to be on what the culture values most, we become discontented, which leads to wanting bigger and more expensive housing. So if we lived by the principle of maximums, how could we handle this issue of housing?

The principle of maximums says you set a limit on the house you will own. This limit could be on square feet but probably a better limit is on how much you will pay for a house. Remember that the size of the house affects your insurance and utilities, so the larger the house you buy, even if it doesn't cost a lot of money to purchase, could affect how much you pay for housing over your lifetime. I'm guessing you are getting this picture. Also, the total cost of continuing to upgrade our housing can equal well over $100,000 in a lifetime that could be given away. Some people will criticize this idea because of the savings from deducting mortgage interest off your taxes. But contributions get the same deduction, will help others at the same time, and increase your heavenly credit.

Setting a maximum and paying off the loan early has another benefit. It is a safeguard from financial disasters and provides tremendous financial freedom. This is one reason I was able to take my first job in education. I took about a 70 percent pay cut to become a college professor but didn't have a mortgage payment. The previous nearly five years, we had been giving 20 to 25 percent of our gross income away, paying an extra $1,000 on our house payment, and not dramatically increasing our standard of living even though my income more than doubled during that period of time. It was only with this financial freedom of not having a mortgage payment that I was able to take the drastic pay cut required to become a college professor.

The overall issue here is setting a maximum for your housing rather than just following our culture. To do this, you need to learn to be content with your housing. Being content will allow you to free up tens of thousands, or even hundreds of thousands, of dollars to give and increase your heavenly account. A couple of things to reiterate: living in a smaller house can also increase community within your family and even in your neighborhood, and while you will probably find it necessary to borrow money to buy your first house, you should pay off that debt as quickly as is practical and avoid the temptation to buy a more expensive house as soon as you have some equity built up in your current house.

Next, we will talk about another area in our lifestyles that can easily become a hindrance to increased generosity. We look at vehicles and transportation.

THINK AND DISCUSS

1. How big is the house you envision you want to own when you are 45 years old? Could you live with a smaller house? Why or why not?

   _____

   _____

2. How old do you want to be when you no longer have house debt? How do you plan to reach that goal?

   _____

   _____

LIVING IT OUT

1. Set a maximum you plan to spend on housing during your lifetime. This will probably mean the most you will spend on buying a house and/or the maximum size of house you will own.

2. If you realize the house you now own is much larger than you need, consider selling your house and buying something smaller to free up money you now spend on mortgage payments, house insurance, and property taxes each year. Redirect that savings into your contribution account.

7.
VEHICLES AND TRANSPORTATION

During the summer of 2016, I went on a mission trip to Belize with one of my daughters. I had lived in Belize for about three months during college but had not returned to the country until that mission trip. The group was actually made up of several smaller groups of people, none of whom knew each other before the week of the trip. One of the smaller groups was a family of six—Dad, Mom, two girls, two boys. They were a neat family. The oldest child in the family was fourteen years old and the youngest about six years old.

When the parents found out this was my fifth child to take on a mission trip and all my older children were out of college, they started asking questions about raising kids. I don't know how much good advice I gave, but I was honored that a psychologist would ask me for advice about raising children! During one of our conversations, the concept of maximums came up and they were intrigued. I explained the concept and they said something like, "We have decided that the nicest type of vehicle we will ever own is a Honda." That is exactly what the concept of maximums is about. It is making a conscious decision about your maximums in all areas of your lifestyle.

When it comes to vehicles, I think there are probably four decisions to make: how much you will spend on vehicles, how long you will keep a vehicle, the utility of the vehicle, and what brand or type of vehicles you will drive which so often relates to pride and status issues. The utility of the vehicle refers to needs you have. Since a lot of our vacations are spent camping with a travel trailer, we own a pickup truck. Most likely, we would not own a truck if we didn't have the camper.

Notice that the family in Belize didn't state how much they would spend on a vehicle but they sort of did. While they probably could afford to drive a luxury vehicle, they were choosing not to spend the extra money on a luxury vehicle when a cheaper, well-made vehicle was enough. They were not being taken in by the status a luxury vehicle would provide.

I had a conversation over lunch about luxury vehicles with a fellow professor at the college where I teach. At the time he was driving a BMW, and I was curious why he chose to drive this make of car. We had a good lunch conversation and I left understanding his thinking much better. He likes nice cars and always had a dream of owning a BMW. He bought it used and believed he got a good deal on the car. A couple of months later, I saw him in a different vehicle, which does not have the same luxury image as a BMW. So, I asked him about it. He said that driving a BMW was causing some image issues he did not wish to portray. So, he sold it. I think he did a good thing. Not that driving a BMW is wrong. But sometimes what we can do and what we should do are different things. Just because we can afford a really nice car doesn't mean we should spend God's money on one.

Our college requires that students attend chapel three days a week. I think most chapels are very good and present some thought-provoking ideas, such as one that took place several years ago by a speaker with a well-known last name who spoke for two or three days. I don't remember all he said, but one concept has stuck with me. He told a story about how he was asked to speak to a Sunday school class at a large church one Sunday. After the service, a young man was assigned to take him out to lunch. When the young man pulled up in new, red, luxury sports car, the young man said something like, "God gave me this car." Our chapel speaker said, "He could have said anything but that. He could have said he was happy he had worked hard, saved, and bought the car. That would have been fine. But to say that God gave him the car means that God loves him more than he loves people who don't have such a car and could never afford one."

I'm sure the young man with the luxury car didn't mean it that way. But it made me think. I have been entrusted with some of God's assets. I have stewardship over those assets. God allows me to use His money the way I want. That doesn't mean God approves of everything I do with His money. It also doesn't mean that if I choose to buy a very expensive car that God gave me that car. It just means I have chosen to use God's resources to buy the car. I wonder how many people would not buy things if they really thought this through better. If we really will give an account for all we do in this life, and I do believe we will need to give that account someday, am I considering this account-giving when I spend God's money?

We took a look at the image piece and practicality issues about vehicles, now let's take a look at the money aspect. Rather than looking at lots of scenarios, we will look at one and you probably can get the idea from there. A couple of sources state that, after the recession beginning in 2008, people now buy about nine cars in a lifetime.[1] That means the average time a vehicle is kept is six to seven years. After you have decided which types of vehicles you won't buy because you have just decided you don't need that type of vehicle, you need to decide how much you will spend on a vehicle. One source claims that you should not spend more than 35 percent of your annual income on a vehicle. That means if you make $50,000 a year, $17,500 is the most you will spend on the vehicle you buy ($50,000 x 0.35). The frugal rule is 10 percent of your annual income and the compromise is 20 percent of your annual income. That doesn't mean you spend this much per year; it means this is the purchase price of your vehicle. For most of us, that means a used vehicle.

New vehicles generally lose value very quickly for a few years. Buying a used vehicle that is between four and ten years old is usually a much better value. While used cars have some repair and upkeep expenses that new cars don't, I have only owned one vehicle where the repair expenses seemed to cost more than the loss of value from what owning a new vehicle probably would have cost. If you research information available on used vehicles such as what Consumer Reports provides, you should find a used vehicle that does not cost a lot in repairs.

If you decide to spend closer to 20 percent of your income on vehicles rather than 35 percent of your income, and buy nine vehicles in your lifetime, the savings would be about $67,500 (9 vehicles x $7,500 – the difference between $17,500 at 35 percent and $10,000 at 20 percent if you make $50,000 per year). If your family makes $100,000 per year, these numbers double and the savings from spending less on vehicles will approach $100,000 in your lifetime. Another issue with less expensive vehicles is the amount of money saved in sales tax, insurance, and licensing costs. Not all states operate the same way with these items, but it is generally much cheaper to insure and license a lower-cost vehicle. Doing so could save $500+ a year in these costs. Over a sixty-year driving lifetime, that is $30,000 saved.

Of course, the total amount saved depends on how long you choose to keep your vehicles. If you decide to buy new vehicles and keep them for twenty years each, you only buy about three in your lifetime. Most people just don't keep a vehicle until it dies. They bail out when there is an expensive repair. The current minivan we drive was bought with about 113,000 miles on it and now has more than 235,000 miles on it. At about 180,000 miles, the transmission went out. After thinking through our options, we replaced the transmission, knowing the van wasn't worth much with a bad transmission. There were no other obvious mechanical issues, the body was still in good shape, and we couldn't get a vehicle even close to as good as our current van for the roughly $3,000 it cost to replace the transmission. We generally keep our vehicles until they die. We hope to drive this van to 300,000 miles. It is now 17 years old and there are a lot of much nicer vehicles on the roads. But we know driving this van is cheaper than getting a newer one, so we keep driving it.

One way we have helped ourselves set maximums for vehicles is to set an amount we save each month toward our next vehicle purchase. When it comes time to buy the next vehicle, we can only spend what is in our vehicle account. When we replaced the transmission in the minivan, it came out of that fund. If we have another large repair to a vehicle, it comes out of that fund. Having this type of fund has helped in a couple of ways. It means we don't borrow money to buy vehicles. It also means we aren't tempted to buy something more expensive that we would regret later. It keeps us from putting too much money toward vehicles and frees up more money to give away. While this type of account might not be for everyone, it is something to consider. Other financial counselors also suggest paying yourself for your next vehicle rather than always borrowing when you buy a vehicle. It means you will need to pay off your current vehicle loan, not let repairs scare you, and begin saving the payment you were making or deciding how much you will save each month toward your next vehicle purchase. Assuming you were able to afford the car payment before, just beginning to save the previous car payment is a good way to save toward your next car.

One question you might want to ask yourself as you decide your maximums with vehicles is, "Would I loan this vehicle to someone?" If the answer is no, or if you are struggling with that thought, you probably have put too much value into your vehicle. If the thought of someone wrecking, denting, or scratching your vehicle is more than you can bear, the vehicle probably means too much to you and just setting maximums isn't the main thing you need to deal with. If everything you own is God's, why wouldn't you loan it to someone? I'm not talking about loaning God's stuff to people who have shown they can't be trusted. I don't think God would want us to loan His stuff to people like that. But if you are struggling to loan out God's stuff to trustworthy people, maybe you haven't yet really taken on the role of a steward. You still think you own it.

During the open comment portion of my dad's memorial service a couple of days after he died, I was struck by one man's story. My dad had loaned his rather new car to this man to take on a trip. I don't recall the reason why the man needed the car, but this was before my dad was married to my mom, so it was a very long time ago and my dad was pretty young. The man somehow dented my dad's car. When this man returned the dented car to my dad, my dad didn't seem too concerned, and it apparently had not affected my dad's relationship with this man. I hadn't known this story, but it must have had a tremendous impact on the man who told it. I really believe my dad understood how a vehicle is something we use and, in the scope of eternity, isn't as important as our relationships with others. I hope you can see vehicles with this understanding, too.

Is there ever a time when owning a luxury car is needed? For most of us, no. I can only think of one situation where owning such a vehicle is needed. If someone has been gifted and called to run a large corporation and the board of directors asks this person to drive a luxury car, it may be needed. God does call some people to live as a Christian witness at a very high level of authority to impact others for Christ. If the board of directors does not require such a vehicle, then a good quality, cheaper vehicle will allow even such a person to be more generous in helping those in need.

If you live in or close to a large metropolitan area, you may be able to meet all of your transportation needs utilizing public transportation and an occasional rental car. I have a cousin who lives in a very large city and she does not own a car. She usually bikes to the train station and rides the train to her work near the center of the city. With the continued development of electric bikes and electric scooters, travel by bicycle or scooter has become easier and requires less physical exertion. I live in a town of about 15,000 people. Our town has an e-bike sharing program. I'm guessing we are unique for a rather small area, but sharing programs are growing and seem to be common in larger cities.

A quick internet search for rental cars shows renting a small car costs less than $40 per day where I live and can even be less in larger cities close to me. If you consider that owning a car costs at least $2,000 per year in depreciation, insurance, and licensing costs, you could rent a car for at least 50 days for $2,000. Deciding to meet your transportation needs without owning a vehicle could free up substantial money to increase your generosity and increase your heavenly account.

For many people, setting maximums for their vehicle use and transportation costs will generate close to, or more than, $100,000 to give away in their lifetime. Being able to set a reasonable maximum will mean having the attitude that God really owns your vehicle and not allowing pride and status to be the reasons behind why you buy the vehicles you do. You will also want to keep vehicles longer, even when they begin to cost money in repairs. As I write this chapter, we are in the Christmas season where vehicle manufacturers work hard to create discontentment. Setting maximums on vehicles means we will learn to be content with what we have or even come up with or utilize creative ways to get around.

Next, I will talk about possessions and how setting maximums on the possessions we own frees up even more money to give.

THINK AND DISCUSS

1. What type of vehicle do you dream of owning? Will that vehicle bring you reward in heaven? Is owning it good stewardship of God's money?

   _____

   _____

2. If you own a vehicle, do you loan it to others if they ask? Why or why not? If you owned your dream vehicle, would you loan it to anyone?

   _____

   _____

LIVING IT OUT

1. If you have vehicle debt and know you could live with a cheaper vehicle, sell your vehicle, pay off the loan, and buy something cheaper. Set up a bank account to save for your next vehicle purchase and redirect some of your savings into your contribution account.

2. Set maximums on the type and cost of vehicles you will drive or transportation alternatives.

3. Investigate your town or city's public transportation or e-sharing alternatives. Try using one or two of these to get familiar with new ways of getting around.

8.
POSSESSIONS
WE BUY

We all need some level of possessions just to live. But how much do we really need and how nice or expensive should these possessions be? There are as many opinions on these questions as there are people, and I won't even try to tell you how you should answer them. But I believe there are some general principles to consider as you decide the answers for yourself. The key question comes down to, "How can I be more generous by setting maximums with my possessions?" This is the exact point of this chapter.

Probably the first thing to consider is who actually owns our possessions. If we believe we actually own the things we possess, we begin to value them more highly than what I believe God intended. And if we aren't careful, we begin to value ourselves based on what we possess instead of who we are in Christ. I know that if I had been overly concerned with nice possessions, I would never have taken the pay cut necessary to become a professor at a Christian college.

Jesus says, "Therefore I tell you, do not worry about your life, what you will eat or drink; or about your body, what you will wear. Is not life more than food, and the body more than clothes?" (Matt. 6:25). I believe Daniel Hillion, author of *Responsible Generosity*, sums it up really well when he says, "We are God's elect and exiles on earth. An exile does not get entangled with many material possessions. He is travelling and may be obliged to move quickly."[1] We have to be careful not to chase nicer possessions to the point where we are not obedient to God's call on our lives. There are some other things we need to consider in addition to setting maximums on the things we possess. Let's take a look at a few of these.

Borrowing and Lending

Larry Burkett used to say that we should all live within our means even if we have to borrow to do it. Anyone who knows his work understands he encourages us not to take on unwarranted debt. So what he really meant was that we shouldn't be buying things we can't afford or don't really need if there is a possibility of borrowing that item from someone else. Sometimes it is way more prudent to borrow what someone else has rather than buy it for ourselves. I think the concept of loaning things to others and asking others if we can borrow something has changed over the past few decades because of the constant marketing bombardment and also a lack of community with our neighbors. The marketers tell us we need things for ourselves, and the thought of even asking if we can borrow something from a neighbor is just too humbling, especially if we don't know the people all that well. Assuming someone trustworthy were to ask if they could borrow an item we own to do a task for themselves, most of us wouldn't even hesitate to loan them the item. If that is true for us, why is it so difficult to ask others if we can borrow something?

As an example, I have borrowed my brother's table saw and power miter saw several times for projects around my property. A few times I have kept them for months as I finished projects. If he needed them back, he would tell me and I always returned them right away when I was done. In turn, he has borrowed a power washer from me a couple of times. The washer was just sitting in my garage and I wasn't using it. I'm glad he feels comfortable asking. I know part of the issue with borrowing comes down to what happens if I break the thing I borrowed. Or what if I loan something and it gets broken? If I see things as God's stuff and not really mine, I don't have as big of a problem when someone else breaks God's stuff. The story told at my dad's memorial service I shared in the previous chapter is a great example of this.

I loaned my pickup truck to someone once so they could carry stones in the bed for a landscaping project. When I got it back, the top of the tailgate had a lot of chips in the paint. Apparently, when they had the stone loaded, some of it hit the tailgate and chipped it. At first, I was sort of miffed. The guy I loaned my truck to hadn't taken as good of care of my truck as I would have liked. As I continued thinking about the situation, though, my thinking began to change. First, my relationship with him was far more valuable than a truck, let alone some chips in the paint. Second, there was no way they could have afforded a truck themselves as their financial situation was not strong. Third, it wasn't really my truck. So, what if it had some chipped paint? It really didn't matter. I'm not even sure he ever knew the paint had been chipped. I decided I was never going to tell him because it just didn't matter much. I'm glad I never said anything to him about it.

Many years ago, I borrowed a couple of power tools from my pastor who had been a carpenter before he became a pastor. I broke one of them. I felt terrible. He didn't ask me to fix the tool, but I fixed it anyway. Fixing it was still cheaper than buying my own tool and I probably wouldn't have ever used that tool again. Borrowing or loaning is not without potential problems, but it is usually much cheaper than buying things we really don't need, which frees up money to be more generous. I have heard of churches that have lists of items and the owners of the items so other church members can borrow things from each other. That sounds like a pretty good idea. People from our church just send out an email asking if anyone has an item. I have loaned out my power washer this way a couple of times. I'm glad to do so.

We also have to consider the issue of convenience and how it affects the purchasing decisions we make. Let's face it—we live in a society of convenience. When we have the need to use something, we want it now! We don't want to wait for a while. I hate lines. Waiting in line can be frustrating. Recently, I needed to visit the local license branch to get some paperwork completed. The line was long, and I ended up waiting for about twenty minutes before an attendant could help me, who I'm pretty sure was the slowest person on their staff. While there were several people to be helped after me, I was the absolute last one to leave their offices that day. I was a little frustrated but, overall, I think I handled the situation pretty well, for me. I can be impatient.

I believe this is one reason we just go ahead and buy stuff rather than borrow. We are generally impatient people. Our society helps create this. We want things *now*! This mindset breeds independence, something I don't believe Jesus taught at all. Jesus taught community and borrowing from each other breeds community.

Identity and Entitlement

"The problem with affluence, then, is not that there is anything wrong with prosperity itself but that material abundance often leads to spiritual amnesia." [2]

There are times when each of us has struggled with a sense of entitlement. We have worked hard at our job, been promoted a few times, and believe we deserve to have this nice thing. But as Christians, we should know that we really deserve to end up in hell, but by God's grace, we don't always get what we deserve! Entitlement is a big deal in our culture, but it is something we really need to get a handle on because it can cause problems for us spiritually.

I'm not saying that we can't own some nice things, but I am saying we have to be aware of when owning nice things becomes problematic. Think of it this way: when we begin to feel better about ourselves based on what we own, we have a spiritual problem. If we feel like we need to own something just to make our lives better, we have a problem. If we know we could live a good life with a $1,000 item but spend $5,000, we could have a problem. If the $1,000 item is good enough for most people, why isn't it good enough for us? Do we believe God loves us more? So often we struggle with a sense of identity in the things that we own, or we believe our nice possessions speak of God's favor on us, but this just isn't true. The good news is that we get to choose how much we spend on possessions and what we want to do with them. Will we use all that we have to get them, and when we get them, will we hold on to them tightly?

I want us to think about how spending the extra $4,000 helps the Kingdom. That is the whole of the message of this book, after all. How can we get to a point where we automatically go there in our decision-making processes? Hillion suggests that the rich Christians in the West should receive help from Christians of developing countries to evaluate our standard of living.[3] Interesting thought. Most of us would probably think that the people living in developing economies just wouldn't understand our way of living. Maybe they understand our way of living a lot better than we do. Sider reminds us that "most rich Christians (and that includes most of us in the Northern Hemisphere) simply do not believe Jesus' teaching about the deadly danger of possessions."[4] When Jesus tells the story of Lazarus and the rich man (Luke 16), He was speaking exactly about this issue. There are so many people living in poverty in our world and we just don't seem to notice. Christians living in developing countries probably have a much better understanding of what is needed to live a good life versus what is just spending money on things we don't really need—money that could be used to help people with real needs instead of spent on our own desires.

Now sometimes owning something we don't necessarily need might make sense, but how can you know? One summer our family of eight went on vacation at a small lake. We owned a pop-up camper and loved to camp. When the trip was over, we all agreed we had a great time but would have had a better time if we could have had access to a boat. So, that fall, we started looking for an older boat. My wife found one and we bought it. It never ran right and the marina bought it back from us after some frustration. We found another older boat the next fall and we bought it for $500 from a marina that was going to sell it to the boat junkyard (I hadn't known there was such a junkyard). We put about $300 in repairs into the boat and used it for close to ten years. We usually go to a family campground for a week each July and that boat was probably the oldest boat docked in the marina that week each year. But it (usually) worked and we had some great family times together with the boat. After our family just got tired of boating, I sold the boat for $1,100. Sure, we had some repairs over the years but it was a great boat for what we paid for it.

So why a boat? I had never really considered owning a pleasure boat, but there were a few considerations where it just made sense for us. Mainly, it came down to the fact that the boat was something our family could do together and we had a seventeen-year span in the ages of our children at the time. All our children could boat together. It fit our family situation well. But I don't believe we needed a $10,000 or $50,000 boat to get the same enjoyment. After owning a boat, I began to realize just how expensive some boats are. We just didn't need an expensive boat. By owning a cheaper, used boat, I was also hoping to train my children that you don't need expensive toys to enjoy life. Cheaper toys usually work quite well, plus if you need an expensive toy to enjoy life or feel better about yourself, you might have a self-image problem. Willmer and Smith say it well, "Christians should find ways to live without expensive luxuries and find ways to do without what other people see as necessities."[5] We would do well to live like this. If your own self-image is based on the nice things that you own, you need to examine your motives—your heart, which is what I will talk about next.

Possessions as a Heart Issue

Beware of the god of money. Did you know there was such a thing? Arthur Simon in his book *How Much Is Enough?* quotes authors McClanen and Stitt who suggest that money becomes Mammon (the god of money) whenever our passion for nice things is stronger than our compassion for the wounded in our world.[6] If I'm honest with myself, that is me most of the time. So, how do I wage the war to keep from needing really nice things? It is a spiritual battle I must constantly fight. It requires a heart of compassion toward those less fortunate. And it requires a desire to sow more into our heavenly account than we put into stuff here on earth. Jesus says this in Matthew 6:19–21,

> "Do not store up for yourselves treasures on earth, where moths and vermin destroy, and where thieves break in and steal. But store up for yourselves treasures in heaven, where moths and vermin do not destroy, and where thieves do not break in and steal. For where your treasure is, there your heart will be also."

Where your treasure is, your heart will be also. That's really it, isn't it? Randy Alcorn's Treasure Principle #2 says, "My heart always goes where I put God's money."[7] So, maybe part of the battle is beginning to buy less stuff and put more money into God's work. Then your heart will follow. While I can't tell you how much you should spend on possessions or how much you should give, one test could be to look at your spending for the past several years. This assumes you are budgeting or at least tracking your spending; if you are not tracking spending, you should start. If you have been spending more on vacations, entertainment, clothes, and so forth, than you are giving away, your heart could be in the wrong place. If you are upgrading things you own before they actually wear out, such as your kitchen, bedroom set, couch, TV, lawn mower, clothes, shoes, and so forth, your heart could be in the wrong place. If you are investing more in the markets than you are giving, your heart could be in the wrong place. I believe your heart does go wherever you put God's money — do you?

So, what now?

If this discussion makes you uncomfortable and you know what God is asking you to do, I encourage you to be obedient and do it. If you are uncomfortable and don't know where to start or what to do, meet with someone you know who is a generous person and get some advice. It might take some searching to find someone because we usually don't know who the generous people are. Often you can tell by how people live. If you have a suspicion someone has a pretty good income but seems like they live below the economic level they could live at, they could be giving a lot of money away. Your pastor might know of some generous people. You may just need to ask God to bring a person to your mind and approach them. Don't put off meeting with someone. If God is nudging you and you don't follow through, Satan is winning. Don't let that happen!

We discuss recreation and entertainment in the next chapter. These are two areas where a lot of money can be spent that could be redirected to help others and increase our heavenly account.

THINK AND DISCUSS

1. Can you be at peace while not having all the "stuff" other people at your income level own? Why or why not?

2. Do you believe loaning things to each other is a good idea? Are there things you are not willing to loan out to others? Why or why not?

LIVING IT OUT

1. Take an inventory of the things you own that you never use. What do you have that you are willing to loan to others?

2. Approach your church leaders to see if they are willing to establish a loaning system for church members. If not, are there people you know who could use some of the things you now own but don't use?

9.
RECREATION AND
ENTERTAINMENT

People who worship health are not healthy. And when we
make pleasure more than a servant, it soon ceases to please.

—Arthur Simon, *How Much Is Enough?*[1]

I have a relative who became a world-class video gamer. At one point, he was ranked in the top ten in the world at this particular game. One problem was that he was in college at the same time, and the game consumed him. Instead of spending time on class assignments, he spent time gaming. While he didn't flunk out of college, his grades were way below his potential and he did get kicked out of an academic program mostly due to his gaming. Another problem was that this became an unhealthy addiction and it took him a few years to regain his spiritual and emotional health. Yes, there is a difference between healthy recreation and unhealthy entertainment.

There are times recorded in the Gospels when Jesus goes away by Himself. It seems that even the Son of God needed to recreate at times. Jesus had a fairly short ministry when compared to how long we will probably work during our lifetime. Most of us will work around 45 years before we stop working for pay. As an aside, I don't believe we have been created to totally stop being productive after we retire. We may not be paid for what we do but being inactive just doesn't seem to keep us healthy. (I talk more about this in the section on retirement.) Learning from my relative in the story above, excessive pursuit of pleasure and self-gratification doesn't seem to be healthy, either.

We should think of recreation as being re-created, which is valuable. When we have been re-created, we feel better. We might not be as grumpy. Our minds think better. We are healthier. Many companies require employees to take vacations. These companies know that taking time off helps make the employee more productive when they are working. It helps them refocus. It renews the mind. This is what it means to be re-created.

But entertainment is not recreation. There is a difference, and our society has moved more and more towards a society of entertainment without recreation. Recreation has the purpose of recreating—of renewing. Entertainment does not. Entertainment is often enjoyable, but it doesn't refresh; in fact, it often does the opposite. I enjoy watching certain sporting events. I enjoy watching certain movies and television shows. But I don't come away from these being renewed or recreated. Sometimes I come away feeling that I have just wasted time and feel guilty, a result of self-gratification. That isn't the purpose of recreation.

How do we know what is recreation and what is entertainment? Well, for starters, I believe true recreation will energize us, not drain us. In general, entertainment fills time but doesn't have an energizing effect on us. We enjoy entertainment, but it doesn't re-create us. Sometimes recreation will cause change in us. We have learned something valuable and are able to implement that into our lives in a productive way. My wife is a good cook and a couple of my daughters enjoy cooking, too. They like to watch cooking shows and learn things that provide encouragement for them to cook better or try new recipes. Cooking shows don't have the same impact on me.

Sometimes recreation will not necessarily encourage change, but it builds relationships. While I don't play video games very often, I have children who spend time playing video games with other people and deepen their relationships using video games. I'm not talking about playing virtually but playing video games together in the same room. And I'm not talking about playing video games that are extremely violent, immodest, or in other ways devalue us as created human beings.

Having explained this some, I don't believe recreation or entertainment is exactly the same for each of us. For example, someone may watch a certain movie and it really moves them to think about life and to act based on the realizations gained from the movie. But that same person can watch another movie and it is just entertaining for them. Most of the movies I watch just end up being entertaining.

Video games may be more easily categorized. I doubt there are many video games that are truly recreating the person playing the game. I will admit I rarely play such games, but I have never found one that wasn't just entertainment. My children love playing board games. We can spend the majority of time during a family get-together just playing board games. I find these harder to categorize between recreation and entertainment. Board games can foster community. They can help develop critical thinking skills. I'm guessing some video games are similar, but I strongly caution against video games and board games that are immodest or embed graphic images in our minds that are the opposite of what Paul encourages in Philippians 4:8. Maybe a good way to look at games is how they build community. If they are not being used to build community, they probably are entertainment and not recreation.

All of us have certain activities and hobbies we like to do but may not meet a recreational need. I love to fish, and fishing is recreating for me. I feel so much more refreshed and energized when I have spent time fishing. But I know fishing doesn't have the same result for everyone; for some it can be extremely tedious or frustrating, which by definition is not re-creational. The point is that you will need to decide for yourself which activities are truly recreating for you and which ones are just entertaining, and of course, some of this will come down to money.

Money Issues Related to Recreation and Entertainment

Recreation and entertainment usually involve money, so let's look at how to set maximums on different types of recreation and entertainment activities, specifically travel, television, and sporting events. The proportion of a family's income going to recreation tends to increase as income increases.[2] Other authors mention this too. It makes sense. The more disposable income we have available, the more we can spend on swimming pools, recreational vehicles, trips, and so forth. I believe we should always ask whether this is how God wants us to spend His money. From my recollection, I have visited 49 of the 50 United States. I haven't made it to Louisiana, but it is on my bucket list. I was about 30 miles away from Louisiana when I biked across the United States in 1982. We biked through Texarkana. If I had known then what I know now, we would have biked south far enough to hit Louisiana!

So, I have traveled within the United States. I was able to visit Hawaii and Alaska with the company I was working for at the time, so that helped. But most of the other states I visited because of extended vacations with our children. They were really good trips; they helped bond us and exposed us and our children to a wonderfully diverse country, but they cost some money. I think it was money well spent. But would I spend that amount of money every year on travel? Nope.

As income increases, many families begin to take more expensive vacations each year without even considering whether they need to spend that amount of money on recreation. Setting maximums on recreational spending means purposefully deciding how much will be spent. This could mean how much will be spent in a year or how often to take a more expensive vacation. Our family handles recreational spending in a similar way to vehicle spending. We have a vacation account we fund each month with automatic bank transfers in the same way we fund our contribution account and our vehicle account. The amount in the vacation account determines what we spend on vacations and other recreation. We don't spend it all each year. It accumulates. To celebrate our 30th wedding anniversary, my wife and I traveled with a group to Israel. It was on our bucket list. It was a great trip, but it wasn't cheap. I'm glad we spent the money. I'm glad we had that amount saved so we could go. We haven't taken a trip like that since. Our plan is to take a more expensive trip to see parts of the world we haven't yet visited about once every five years.

For us, this is a good compromise. Why not take a more expensive vacation with a purpose about every five years? The other years, we can take a less expensive vacation. We have to remember our goal—to free up money to be more generous. For example, if you are spending $5,000 per year on vacations, why not do that every five years and spend $2,000 the other years? I'm not trying to tell you how much to spend but giving an example. The $3,000 you save the other four years equals $12,000 you could give away every five years. If you add this up over forty years of work, that is $96,000 (40 years / 5 years = 8 x $12,000).

Most of us don't spend $5,000 every year on vacations and recreation. But maybe you spend $2,000 and could cut that back some. More people are taking "stay-cations" instead of leaving home. If planned well, these could actually be more "re-creational" than going away on vacation. I don't know about you, but at times I come home from extended or busy vacations needing a vacation! I know I'm not alone in this.

Another area that many Americans rely heavily on for entertainment purposes is the TV. But have you ever really considered the entertainment value for what it costs? Let's assume cheap cable TV costs about $30 per month. If you give up cable as a way to manage entertainment, you would save $400 per year (including taxes). Over forty years, that equals $16,000. Given that the average cable package is reported closer to $60 per month, this means the savings would be double that, or over $30,000, in forty years. We have never paid for cable TV. We only get the channels that are available for free. Sure, we miss some shows and sporting events we want to watch, but we don't really feel like we missed out. I doubt I will die regretting not having cable.

A couple of times a year, we put our TV away. We unplug it and put it somewhere that isn't easily accessed. I go through withdrawal for a couple of weeks and then really start to enjoy the time spent without our TV. It might sound crazy, but I am more purposeful with my time. I read more. I get more sleep. We play more games as a family. We all use our time in more meaningful ways. I don't go to bed feeling like I have just wasted a couple of hours watching meaningless shows.

One last example—sporting events. Every other year or so I bring up the issue of gambling in one of my classes. I ask students if they think gambling is a waste of money. (I think it is but I don't tell them this until after we have discussed it, not to mention that gambling can be dangerously addictive.) Almost every student says gambling is a waste of money. I next ask them if they believe buying season tickets to a major college's sports season is a waste of money. The young men in the class typically respond that spending this money is not a waste of money. Most of the young women in the class usually don't say anything. I live pretty close to South Bend, Indiana, where the University of Notre Dame is located. The cost of season tickets to Notre Dame football (including the cost of the tickets and the required donation to be considered for tickets) ranges from $1,150 to $4,200. Most of us don't attend sports events alone, so that would be between $2,300 and $8,400 for two season tickets. Why is it that we believe someone who takes a set amount of money and chooses to gamble with it for entertainment is viewed negatively, but someone who spends a large sum of money on season tickets is not viewed negatively? Both are seeking entertainment. Two "cheap" season tickets to see Notre Dame football over forty years is $92,000 and that isn't considering inflation. Plus, that money is completely gone! With gambling, there is at least some chance of getting some of it back, but I still don't recommend it.

I don't want to leave the impression that we should never do anything entertaining. I just want us to think about whether spending the money is worth the long-term cost. I have been to athletic events. I believe they were worth the money. I truly believe Jesus would have gone to some athletic events and wouldn't have criticized the person who invited Him to attend. It would have been a way for Jesus to spend time with people. But the main point is that there would have been a purpose to attending. Entertainment with the purpose of spending time with people could be good time and money well spent.

The purpose of this chapter is not to tell you what to do, but to get you thinking if you are spending money on recreation and/or entertainment that isn't necessary. In a society such as ours, one where we don't have to work twelve hours a day just to survive, we have a lot more free time than in many other countries. I believe we need to continually ask ourselves whether we are spending this time wisely and frugally. Are we being re-created or just entertaining ourselves? Do we use our time to build community or just spend money on activities that leave us empty? I like what Sutherland and Nowery say, "When we live in primary consideration of Him, gratitude minimizes our tendencies to squander our resources on self-gratification."[3]

The next chapter discusses setting maximums on saving for retirement and on other investments. Our world's thinking is to save all we can in this life, which discourages generosity. We will see how setting maximums on the amount we save allows us to be far more generous and increase our heavenly account.

THINK AND DISCUSS

1. After reading this chapter, are you comfortable with the amount of money you spend on recreation and/or entertainment? What do you believe you need to change?

_____

_____

_____

2. Do you believe the way you currently spend vacation time and money is re-creating? What type of activities re-create you?

_____

_____

_____

LIVING IT OUT

1. Plan how you can save money you now spend on vacations, recreation, and entertainment. Redirect the savings into your contribution account.

2. Open a recreation account at your bank. Begin to fund the account systematically and only spend the amount you put into this account for vacations, recreation, and entertainment.

10.
RETIREMENT
AND INVESTING

Retirement seems to be a relatively new concept. Howard Dayton points out, "Scripture gives no examples of people retiring."[1] In our wealthy society, many people have the ability to save enough money so they are usually able to spend some time at the end of their lives not working even when they still have some ability to work. Our society applauds those who are able to achieve retirement at a relatively young age. For many people, retirement has become their primary goal in living. They live for retirement.

Living for retirement generally means we fixate on saving as much as possible so we can retire. Of course the earlier we plan to retire, the more we need to save quickly so we can have enough to live on during retirement. Saving more means giving less away. We are building bank accounts and investment accounts instead of building a heavenly credit. This is a very worldly way to live. Ben Witherington III in his book *Jesus and Money* says this: "But the connection between work, life, ministry, and Christian behavior requires more careful thought. If the purpose of making money now is so one can live in luxury and idleness later, that is *not* a Christian motivation."[2]

In *End-Times Money Management*, Gary Moore requotes a 1997 article posted in the *Philadelphia Inquirer* ("In Pursuit of Wealth, Christians Have Forgotten Biblical Teachings," *Philadelphia Inquirer* [January 15, 1997]), "In pursuit of wealth and worldly possessions,

Christians have become virtually indistinguishable from the rest of the world. We have bought into non-Christian precepts. Note the irony: Christians seeking and encouraging others to seek that which our Lord repeatedly warned against."[3] This article is speaking to the issue of wanting to get rich, which Paul warns about in 1 Timothy 6.

So, how do we keep our societal thinking at bay and pursue a biblically-based way of approaching retirement? I believe we do this by setting maximums. Dayton says, "I would like to suggest a radical antidote for the potential disease of loving money: *Determine a maximum amount of savings and investments that you will accumulate and stop there.*"[4] The reality is that our medical profession has the ability to keep us alive a lot longer than was the case generations ago. Many of us will outlive our ability to be productive in the current job we hold. Right now, in the United States, we still have Social Security, which helps us when we can no longer generate an income. But relying on Social Security probably isn't a good idea. For one thing, it usually isn't enough to both live on and pay for unexpected expenses. For another thing, our government is in extreme debt, which will create either the need to decrease Social Security payments in the future, or print money, which will cause inflation and make what we get from Social Security worth a lot less than it is worth today. In either case, the purchasing power of Social Security will decrease. Because of this, it seems prudent to save some money for retirement.

But how much should we save? I believe there is one overriding principle. If we save enough to live a modest lifestyle in old age (perhaps to 85 or 90 years old), we have saved enough. I can't tell you how much that really is because it depends on what you decide is a modest lifestyle and also where you live. The cost of living is different in various regions of the country. But I know that continuing to save when you have enough to provide for yourself is not biblical. This is not the same advice many Christian financial counselors give. Some of them give you a percentage to save and encourage you to never stop saving that percentage no matter how large your investment account becomes. This advice is often given with the idea that you will be able to give away so much more in the future if you continue to invest. But also remember that saving more provides a larger commission to the advisor as most advisors receive a percentage of your account balance each year, so the advice to save and not give now may be self-serving to the advisor.

But other Christian writers have different advice. For example, Larry Burkett says, "I believe that as the economy crumbles, it will not be possible to hoard. Those who have been storing up wealth in contemplation of things unknown, retirement, or the better life, will be greatly disappointed when it is all consumed like so much chaff and fodder."[5] Speaking of generosity, Andy Stanley in his book *How to be Rich* says, "If you wait until you're rich, you'll never start, because rich people live in denial that they're rich."[6] Referring to Jesus' and Paul's teachings, Blomberg suggests there seem to be extremes of wealth and poverty that are intolerable in the Christian community.[7]

By setting reasonable maximums on how much we will accumulate, we fight against the desire to be rich and we keep our dependence on God. When it comes right down to it, we are already rich when compared to much of the world. America's most generous zip codes aren't its richest zip codes. As wealth increases, people become more insulated and isolated.[8] This doesn't seem to be a biblical mindset—to become more insulated and isolated. But when we become rich, fear of losing wealth kicks in, skepticism about the motives of others toward us kicks in, and we tend to isolate ourselves from others. As we become wealthier, we are insulated from many financial stresses that others with less savings experience. The more wealth we have, the more we don't need community. I don't see how this, in any way, reflects the heart of God. Even the Trinity reflects community: the forms of God interacting together and representing different gifts among God's people. When we isolate ourselves from the church, we are not able to help each other as was the experience of the church in Acts. Jacques Ellul says it this way, "Either our confidence is in God or it is in our savings account. To claim that we can thus insure ourselves and still put our trust in God is to add hypocrisy to mistrust of God."[9]

When it comes to some basic concepts on saving and investing, I think Dave Ramsey's initial methods are a good place to begin. Start with saving a basic emergency fund of $1,000 or a little more and put it into a basic savings account at a bank or credit union. Pay off debt that isn't mortgage debt and continue to build up a fund of three to six months of living expenses in case you lose a job or have an unplanned major financial event. If your company has a retirement plan, usually a 401(k) or 403(b), and matches your contributions into the account, begin putting the maximum of what the company matches into the account if you can afford to contribute that much.

I believe that getting out of all debt, except mortgage debt, should take precedent over putting money into retirement. Many financial advisors won't give this advice. They will say that investing is more important than paying off debt because the markets can earn so much more. But what they usually won't tell you is you could lose a lot when the markets do poorly and still have the debt. I believe you are always wiser to pay off the debt first and then begin to invest.

After you are out of all debt, except your mortgage, making payments to yourself for a car fund and potentially a vacation account, investing in a retirement account, and paying extra on your mortgage every month, then start to give more than the tithe at the same time. You need to pray about this and decide how much each of these should be. "God can produce far greater returns on money invested in heaven today than Wall Street or real estate ever can."[10] One of the questions that you need to ask yourself is if you are willing to die with a lot of money in investments but almost nothing in your heavenly account. I believe that would be tremendously embarrassing as you give an account of your life to God. This is basically what Jesus is teaching against in Luke 12:16–21. The rich man in this passage dies with a lot of wealth accumulated in this life as he prepares for a better future. He has an abundant harvest, so he decides to store (save) more by building bigger barns. But he dies without either using the wealth to help others or even enjoying it himself.

My wife and I have set a maximum amount we will accumulate in retirement and other savings. Once that maximum is reached, we will still put money into the retirement account to get the company match, but we will also pull the excess out of the account and give it away. To avoid penalty, you need to be at least 59½ years old when you start this strategy. I will easily be 59½ when we hit our agreed retirement account maximum, if we ever hit the maximum. I probably started saving for retirement later than I should have. If we need to live only on the retirement savings after I stop being paid to work, we can probably fund ourselves until at least 85 years of age and maybe a little longer. If we run out of money, our children will need to help, but I doubt that we will run out before we die. We can always adjust our lifestyle if needed.

I plan to continue working when I am no longer paid. Volunteering for organizations who need accounting help or other skills I possess would be a good way to use time and energy during the later years in my life. One man at our church is a carpenter by trade. He is more than 70 years old but works almost every day building houses for the local Habitat for Humanity. I really admire him. He could be sitting around in retirement, but he has chosen to use his time to help others. I believe he is building his heavenly account. He is using what skills he has to gain friends on earth and both friends and funds in heaven. I hope my body holds out well enough so I can do something similar. It might not be Habitat for Humanity but providing housing for others would be a good way to spend retirement.

Burkett says it this way, "There is nothing wrong with saving in moderation for retirement. But there is something wrong with storing unnecessarily, believing that is the only way to provide for later years."[11] Set a maximum retirement account and a maximum for other investing or savings accounts. Fund it systematically and be generous while you are funding these accounts. It is a good strategy to keep from falling into the trap of wanting to get rich.

Tables 3–5 below show how much savings can grow if you begin saving early. You really don't need to save much for the investments to grow to a sizable amount before you stop investing. These tables assume you never make more than $50,000 per year but that you invest for forty-five years. Most of us have incomes that grow to more than $50,000 during our lives, so this example should be a low estimate. The stock market has historically returned about 7 percent since the Great Depression. I started investing in my retirement accounts in 1988 and my average return has been almost exactly 7 percent during that time. I have invested more conservatively than many people, so I probably could have achieved a higher average return, but my wife and I are comfortable with the way our retirement funds are invested. Being comfortable with how you invest is extremely important.

Table 3
Future Value of Investment Savings at 5% Rate of Return

Annual income	$50,000	$50,000	$50,000	$50,000	$50,000	$50,000
Percent invested	5.00%	6.00%	7.00%	8.00%	9.00%	10.00%
Rate of return	5.00%	5.00%	5.00%	5.00%	5.00%	5.00%
Number of years	45	45	45	45	45	45
Future Value	$399,250	$479,100	$558,951	$638,801	$718,651	$798,501

Table 4
Future Value of Investment Savings at 7% Rate of Return

Annual income	$50,000	$50,000	$50,000	$50,000	$50,000	$50,000
Percent invested	5.00%	6.00%	7.00%	8.00%	9.00%	10.00%
Rate of return	7.00%	7.00%	7.00%	7.00%	7.00%	7.00%
Number of years	45	45	45	45	45	45
Future Value	$714,373	$857,248	$1,000,123	$1,142,997	$1,285,872	$1,428,747

Table 5
Future Value of Investment Savings at 8% Rate of Return

Annual income	$50,000	$50,000	$50,000	$50,000	$50,000	$50,000
Percent invested	5.00%	6.00%	7.00%	8.00%	9.00%	10.00%
Rate of return	8.00%	8.00%	8.00%	8.00%	8.00%	8.00%
Number of years	45	45	45	45	45	45
Future Value	$966,264	$1,159,517	$1,352,770	$1,546,022	$1,739,275	$1,932,528

As you can see from these tables, you should have plenty saved if you continue investing and start young. These numbers do not consider any matching funds from an employer, so you could have substantially more saved when including any employer match. Set a maximum for the amount you will save. When you hit that maximum, begin giving the excess away.

Ultimately, the issues of how large of a savings account to keep, how much to save towards retirement, and how much to be giving during the time you are saving toward retirement are issues of where you put your trust. If you trust God to provide for you should some unforeseen event happen, you will save less and be able to give more. If you are trusting in yourself, fear takes over and you will believe you need to save as much as possible. If you live in fear, you will not be giving generously and not be increasing your heavenly account. You will probably die with a lot of money saved on earth and almost no credits to your account in heaven. That is not what we want.

The next chapter explores the issue of inheritances, which will help you set maximums for how much to leave behind. In Bible times, leaving an inheritance had the purpose of providing a way for your children to earn a living. We look at how education relates to inheritance today.

THINK AND DISCUSS

1. How do you plan to spend your time after you quit working for pay?

   _____

   _____

   _____

2. As you think about saving for retirement and investing, do you fear you won't have enough? What does this say about your trust in God as our provider?

   _____

   _____

   _____

LIVING IT OUT

1. After prayer, thought, and seeking advice, set a maximum for the amount of money you will save for retirement.

2. Begin saving an emergency fund of three to six months of expenses and stop depositing into this fund once you reach this amount.

11.
INHERITANCE
AND EDUCATION

"A good person leaves an inheritance for their children's children,
but a sinner's wealth is stored up for the righteous."
—Proverbs 13:22

This proverb is often used to make the case for perpetuating wealth for future generations. It implies the need to give enough inheritance money to our children so plenty would be left over for our grandchildren. Such reasoning seems to be behind some Christian financial counselors' advice when they encourage clients to continue investing when really the client already has plenty of money for their own retirement. It is so their children will receive large sums of money, continue investing this money, and perpetuate wealth for future generations. While I don't believe it is wrong to give some wealth to our children or even our grandchildren, I want to suggest there are differences between biblical times and today, which might cause you to view the purpose of inheritance a little differently.

In *Rich Christians in an Age of Hunger*, author Ron Sider explains, "Land was the basic capital in early Israel's agricultural economy, and the land seems to have been divided in such a way that each extended family had the resources to produce the things needed for a decent life."[1] In other words, in Israel, most of the inheritance was land, which was needed to earn a decent living. Sider also writes, "families possessed resources to earn a living that would have been considered reasonable and acceptable, not embarrassingly minimal. That is not to suggest that every family had exactly the same income. It does mean, however, that every family had an equality of economic opportunity up to the point that they had the resources to earn a living that would enable them not only to meet minimal needs of food, clothing, and housing but also to be respected participants in the community."[2]

Of course, each individual was able to decide whether they would work hard and use their resources wisely. If they did not, they might have to sell the land, which ultimately resulted in selling themselves into slavery.

If a person did not handle his share of the land properly and needed to sell the land and himself into slavery, God had provided for this unfortunate situation by establishing the concept of Jubilee, which would return the land back to the original family in no more than fifty years. It was a good concept. Every generation or so the land went back to the original owner allowing for the family to maintain a way to generate a living. We don't know if Jubilee was ever practiced, but the intent of inheritance seems to be one of providing the ability to earn a basic living.

Times have certainly changed. People often died younger in Old Testament times than today, so more people today receive their inheritance when they are in their sixties. There are still family farms, but most of us are no longer living an agricultural lifestyle. Most children leave their parents sometime in their twenties and have thirty or even forty years to earn a living and generate their own resources before their parents die. "Usually the children are already well-established financially when the parents die. The children can hardly be said to be in 'need' of a large estate."[3]

There are some exceptions. Some people have health issues or experience disasters that leave them struggling financially and it is not their fault. Some become pastors or missionaries and are not well cared for financially by the church, mission organization, or other support groups. These people could probably benefit from a larger inheritance. But most people who "need" money in their sixties have not been wise financially during their lives. They may have bought on credit and spent a lot of God's money paying interest instead of waiting until they could really afford to buy something. They may still be making mortgage payments as they approach retirement because they bought a more expensive house than they needed or could easily afford. If you were acting as steward of a large estate, would you give a large inheritance to the child of the original owner of the estate when that child spent about forty years wasting money already? I doubt it. So, as God's steward, should you give a lot of money to your own child who spent a lifetime wasting money?

If you want to be sure the wealth God has allowed you to accumulate during your lifetime will be used for His work, you need to give it away while you are alive or at your death instead of giving it all to your children. I realize there are many investment managers who will suggest that giving to your children will allow the wealth to grow more so there is more to give away. But there is also the possibility that the markets or other investments will totally fail and all that wealth will be lost, none of it given to God's work. If you really want to invest in your heavenly account, give it away before you die, or designate in your will where the money is to be given at your death. This way you are certain it will be used for Kingdom work.

I want to propose a different way to look at inheritance. If the biblical inheritance was providing what your children needed so they could earn a living, what is today's equivalent? I think the answer is education. In our society, people need a level of education to have the ability to earn a decent living. This isn't always a college education. Some people are really gifted with their hands and may be better at laying bricks, building houses, or fixing cars than the rest of us. These people may need to attend a trade school. But for most children, being able to earn a decent living probably means some level of college education. Providing for your children to attend college may be the best inheritance you can leave to them.

In Bible times, children could squander their inheritance. We saw earlier what would happen if landowners didn't work the land well and couldn't provide for themselves—they would have to sell the land and go into slavery. It wasn't God's intention, but it happened. The same is true today. Children don't always apply themselves in college or after college and struggle financially. It might be really tempting to continue to help this child while he or she basically wastes his or her life. I don't believe giving such a child more money is helping them at all. Sometimes the things that help us the most are when we have to take responsibility for our actions and mistakes. As a parent of seven children, I know how hard it can be to watch a child struggle financially. It tears you up. You just want to step in and give them money. But that won't help them. What they need is your prayer and willingness to be there if they ask for advice. Continuing to bail them out financially will only allow them to put off really growing up.

College education is getting more and more expensive. I earn my living from teaching college and even I think college is expensive. It can be a huge sacrifice for some parents to make sure their children can attend college. I am not trying to lay a guilt trip on parents. I don't believe that giving your children the inheritance of a college education means paying for the entire thing. It means making sure they can get to college. It also doesn't mean attending a Christian college, even though I believe there can be lasting value in attending one. I have a cousin who called me a couple of years ago and was struggling with the extra cost of his daughter attending a Christian college. He wanted my help understanding whether the extra cost was worth it. We talked for a while and then I asked him what it was worth to him for his daughter to be instructed in a Christian mindset that would last for the next sixty-plus years. I hadn't gone into the conversation knowing I would ask that question, but it seemed right at the time. It didn't take him very long to think that through. His daughter went to a Christian college.

Not everyone will be able to afford a Christian college or even a state university. But almost everyone can afford to attend a junior college or a regional state college. Sometimes students are even paid to attend these colleges when all their scholarships come through. I believe some level of college education is available to almost everyone in the United States. Perhaps the best inheritance you can give your children is to help them work hard during high school, study well for their SAT or ACT, and earn as much scholarship money as possible.

My wife and I have told our children that we will make sure they can attend college if they want to go. We aren't paying for all of it and have made them take financial responsibility for their education. But we have loaned money when needed, let them live at home for free during the summer and during the school year if they want, and provided some other things that ensure they can attend college. We expect them to have a job during college, too. Having a job for a few hours a week helps minimize loans and encourages our children to use their time more efficiently than many college students use their time. I don't think any of my children missed out on anything really important by having a job during college. One of our sons ran track and cross country during college and still worked a few hours a week. Our oldest daughter was in theatre during college and worked a few hours a week. They both had decent GPAs. Not a 4.0 GPA but, as a college professor, I know that getting all A's is overrated unless you are trying to get into a prestigious graduate school after college. They both knew how to manage their time and work hard. Those two skills are probably two of the most important skills for all of life, not just during college.

Some families believe strongly in Christian K-12 education. Three of our children should graduate from a local Christian school and four of our children graduated from the local public high school. In some cases, Christian K-12 education costs more per year than Christian college education costs and probably costs more over the combined twelve to thirteen years than college will cost. It depends on scholarships at both levels of education. I believe there is value to Christian K-12 education, but most families cannot afford to send their children to Christian K-12 and then help their children through college. We could not have afforded to send all seven of our children to Christian elementary and secondary schools. So, this is something you will need to decide as a family. One of our sons graduated from the local Christian secondary school but we didn't have the money to pay all his costs to attend. He needed to work jobs to help pay for this cost. We did not force or ask him to attend this school. He wanted to attend. While he was busy, he managed his time well and was still able to play sports during the summer and the school year and have a job.

There are many ways we hope to give our children an inheritance that extends way past our grandchildren. Kreider says, "Leaving great wealth to children can deaden the talents and energies of the children."[4] Our children know they should receive a modest amount of money when my wife and I die unless all our assets have been used up before then. But the amount they will receive is a maximum amount, not a minimum. Most of our estate is to be given away when we die. We have some organizations named. If we should die before all our children are through college, their college education is provided for first before the rest of the money is split up. This serves a couple of purposes. It makes sure our children know that, even if by some unusual circumstance our estate gets quite large, they will not get the bulk of the estate. They need to take financial responsibility for themselves. It also lets them know we value their education and we will be sure they can attend college if they want, even if we are dead before they can attend college. It also shows that we value the credit in our heavenly account more than we value the balance in our own bank account or in their bank accounts, which brings me to another kind of inheritance that lasts longer.

Not all inheritance is monetary. As a Christian, I believe the most important inheritance I can give is a spiritual foundation. By faithfully modeling a Christian walk to my children, I have given them an inheritance that should extend to my children's children and far beyond. As Peter declares in 1 Peter 1:7, this spiritual inheritance is of greater worth than money. In Acts 20:32–35, Paul talks about the spiritual inheritance he leaves with the Ephesians. When we strive to leave a large monetary inheritance to our children, we may undermine the much greater value of a spiritual inheritance.

Because financial disasters do happen, the next chapter will explore how we can overcome financial disasters by using maximums to manage our finances.

THINK AND DISCUSS

1. Do you believe education today is comparable to the giving of land to the next generation in Bible times? Why or why not?

   _____

   _____

   _____

2. Do you hope your parents leave you a large inheritance? What does this attitude say about the condition of your heart?

   _____

   _____

   _____

LIVING IT OUT

1. Begin living as if you will not receive an inheritance when your parents die. Decide what you will do with the money if your parents leave you an inheritance.

2. Meet with an attorney or other financial planner to create a will for what to do with your money when you die. Decide how much you will give your children when you die. Talk with your children about this so they are aware and know why you have made this decision.

12.
PLANNING FOR
FINANCIAL DISASTERS

*"Does the same Christ who said we should look to the birds
and the lilies and trust our heavenly Father to provide for
our futures and that we are to lay up treasures in heaven
and not on earth, really want us to stockpile gold bullion
and store up years of freeze-dried food in a bomb shelter?"*

—Randy Alcorn[1]

This is a great question.

I was giving a talk about maximums and generosity at Grace College. I often title these talks, "The Case for Voluntary Christian Socialism." It is a catchy title and creates interest. Basically, it means that we voluntarily meet the needs of others by sharing what we have. In some small way, we try to generate more equality in our Christian society than happens automatically, like the church in Acts where people are selling things they don't really need and sharing with others. During the question time, one young lady asked about financial disasters. Shouldn't we save so that if something bad happened financially, we would have enough to take care of ourselves?

It is a fair question and one our culture struggles with. We are taught to make sure we save enough so that if a financial disaster happens to us, we have the resources needed to take care of ourselves.

I don't see much basis for this thinking in the Old Testament and no basis for this thinking at all in the New Testament. What we are doing when we hoard finances is starting to protect rather than provide. Larry Burkett cautions against such thinking. While providing for ourselves and our family is scriptural and addressed both in the Old and New Testaments, trying to protect ourselves from anything that might happen is not.[2] It is a sign of fear. Platt says it this way, "The core issue is do we trust God?"[3]

I do believe God has an answer to the young woman's question and that answer is the church. Just as in Acts, when people are selling possessions and giving to those in need, the church today should be willing to do the same. When a family comes under severe financial difficulty, those in the church who have excess resources should be willing to help. "If anyone of you has material possessions and sees a brother or sister in need but has no pity on them, how can the love of God be in you?" (1 John 3:17–18). "Wishing someone well without offering any help illustrates a 'vacuous' faith."[4] I believe it is the responsibility of the church to help members in need. If you don't trust your church to help, you probably are attending the wrong church.

Let me be clear that this doesn't mean we irresponsibly spend all the money we make, not have an emergency savings fund, and totally rely on others to bail us out if we hit financial difficulty. I do believe the church should help this type of person but more with accountability and training than with continually funding their poor financial behaviors. If all of us spent all our money, there wouldn't be any of us with resources to help others. It can be difficult to know when to help others who have financial difficulties, especially when they always seem to have financial difficulties. Close relationships in the church help. If we really don't know each other well, knowing when to help financially and when to just counsel and encourage will be difficult.

Our church has a benevolence fund specifically to be used to help people in financial need. Sometimes the needs are greater, and the church urges us to contribute more to the fund. But there are times in our church when people help each other outside of the benevolence fund. Our pastor shared with me that there was a time when so many people were helping one family and giving the money to the pastor to pass on to them that our pastor was reaching the allowed federal maximum gift limit for the year, which was $14,000. Healthy churches help each other. Sometimes this means money is given by the local church to help, and sometimes this will come from the broader church body as we help others in need.

First Timothy 5:8 says, "Anyone who does not provide for their relatives, and especially for their own household, has denied the faith and is worse than an unbeliever." This verse clearly states we should be helping our own family members when financial difficulties arise. When our daughter Rebecca was in the hospital more than 100 miles from our home for months at a time, many people helped us financially. But some of the most helpful provision was when relatives and church friends cared for our children when we needed to spend time at the hospital learning how to care for our daughter. I believe such financial and other support was a great testimony to both us and others who were watching our life during that time. In similar ways, we have helped other family members when they have hit unexpected financial difficulties. Sometimes we knew the other family members could have found enough money to pay their own unexpected expense but giving them some money to help during this unexpected time was both good for them and good for us. It helped to bond us together more.

Until I was about 15, the church I grew up in did not have a full-time pastor. There was a teaching elder and he was paid some but not enough to allow him to pastor full-time. Every quarter, following a carry-in meal, we had a "business meeting" on a Sunday afternoon. The meeting was to discuss any issues the elders wanted to bring before the church, but it was also to decide where to give the excess money generated the previous quarter. I don't remember a quarter where there was ever a shortage of money.

The church began to grow and then something happened that reminds me of Israel. People started asking for a "king," a full-time pastor. We grew big enough that we could afford a full-time pastor. Some older people in the church warned against this but the vote ultimately passed, and the church hired a full-time pastor.

One of the first things the pastor did was to stop giving excess money away each quarter. He didn't believe giving the excess away was a good idea. Some in the church disagreed but the suggestion was passed by the congregation. Within a couple of years, the church had split. I was in college when the split happened, so I don't know all the exact reasons. The church, which had been both spiritually and financially healthy, was broken. Looking back, I truly believe part of the church split related to no longer putting complete trust in God's provision and beginning to rely on financial reserves.

I am not trying to say the model of church I had growing up should be every church's model. But protecting rather than providing leads to no longer trusting God, which is dangerous. Perhaps a church needs to have some financial reserves, but there should be a maximum amount for that. Like Jacques Ellul says, "Either our confidence is in God or it is in our savings account. To claim that we can thus insure ourselves and still put our trust in God is to add hypocrisy to mistrust of God."[5]

You might be asking how your church can even help the needy because it seems like it barely meets budget anyway. If believers generally gave their first 10 percent to their local church, most churches would have so much money they would be able to start giving money away. I think churches should basically operate under the same principle of maximums. There should be maximums set on where the church will spend its money. This would mean maximums on staff, facilities, materials, and so forth. There would be savings set aside to provide for special needs that come up, but probably not enough to protect from every disaster that could happen. Once the maximum reserves have been met, the excess would be able to be given to other needy organizations and to fund missions work. I believe the next chapter about where to give should help answer additional questions for this issue and more.

THINK AND DISCUSS

1. What emotions does the term "Voluntary Christian Socialism" stir up in you? Do you believe you have a responsibility to help other Christians in need?

_____

_____

_____

2. Do you currently attend a church that you trust to help you if a financial disaster strikes?

_____

_____

_____

LIVING IT OUT

1. If your church does not have a fund to help church members in need, approach your church leadership about establishing such a fund.

2. Is there anyone in your immediate family with a financial need that you can meet? If so, how will you approach them?

13.
WHERE TO GIVE

*"So when you give to the needy, do not announce it
with trumpets, as the hypocrites do in the synagogues
and on the streets, to be honored by others. Truly I
tell you, they have received their reward in full."*

—Jesus, Matthew 6:2

The above Scripture lends perspective to this chapter. We learn much
about giving from this passage, such as to whom we should give,
what our attitudes should be, and even why we give. While part of
this passage instructs us to not proudly tell others about our giving
(attitude), there is one word we often miss—*when.* Jesus assumed
His followers would give; He expected people to help others by giving. Because of this passage and many others, we know giving is
important to God. It's a matter of when, not if. But this chapter also
takes a look at *where* to give, which gets at the heart of God.

From an earlier discussion on tithing in this book, we also know
God cares about how much to give. I believe we should be viewing
the tithe (10 percent) as a minimum amount we give, not a maximum, but many of us have this backward. Living a lifestyle of maximums frees up more to give than a tithe, which if you recall, giving
builds your heavenly account. I agree with Powell who says,

"Personally, I think that all the reasons why tithing would
be a greater imposition in our era than it was in biblical

times need to be considered within the context of one ines-
capable fact: we live in a time of incredible affluence. Most
Christians in America could give away a lot more than one
tenth of their income (gross income, before taxes) and still
be wealthy beyond the wildest dreams of Israelite farmers or
Galilean fishermen."[1]

So true.

God also cares about the spreading of the gospel message to the
world (Matt. 28:19). Should this impact where we give? I would
think so. I firmly believe that if committed Christians gave their first
10 percent to the local church, the broader, worldwide church could
have reached the entire world for Christ already. I have no proof for
this except, as I showed earlier in this book, each additional one percent of giving generates approximately five billion more dollars per
year. Increasing from a three percent of income giving level that most
surveys find Christians give to a 10 percent giving level would generate at least $35 billion more per year. As long as local churches didn't
just spend this on more staff and facilities, $35 billion more per year
would fund about 280,000 more missionaries at a $125,000 per year
support level, which is the reported average needed for a missionary
family per year. If the local church would receive 10 percent and set
maximums on the church's own spending, there would be tremendous amounts leftover to reach the world for Christ.

But if all that $35 billion or so went to fund missionaries, I think
the church would still not be doing all that Jesus said to do in respect to giving. Jesus said a lot about helping the poor, the "needy."
Matthew 25 is where we find the story of the sheep and the goats.
Jesus says that when we don't help the poor, we identify with the
goats and are not welcomed into the kingdom (vv. 31–46). In Luke
16, Jesus also tells the story of Lazarus and the rich man. The rich
man ends up in hell because he isn't willing to help the poor man,
Lazarus, who lived right outside the rich man's gate (vv. 19–31).
We know helping the poor is important to Jesus, but it seems to be
important for us as well. Blomberg adds, "If most affluent Western
Christians were to be honest about the extent of their surplus, they
would give considerably higher than 10 percent to Christian causes.

And given the paltry percentages of most church budgets that help the materially needy, locally or globally, they would make sure that a substantial percentage of their giving went directly to individuals and organizations that offer holistic salvation of body and spirit to the desperately poor throughout the world."[2] I find it interesting that the well-known singer, Bono, has a similar perspective about helping the poor. He said in a YouTube video, "God is with the vulnerable and poor. God is with us if we are with them. Get involved in what God is doing because it is already blessed."[3] He has the right idea.

The church in Acts seems to have the right idea, too. In the Acts church, people were selling excess assets and sharing the proceeds with others who needed help. Sider addresses the topic of the poor and how to help them most effectively; he believes the most effective strategy to reduce poverty is to provide clean water, de-worming treatments for children, and insecticide-treated bed nets to prevent malaria-carrying mosquitoes from biting people in their sleep.[4]

Helping the poor is not necessarily best accomplished by just giving them money. It is best accomplished by helping them provide for themselves. Oftentimes, so much time and energy are spent in poor communities just accessing and carrying water that families don't have time for other productive labor. Disease devastates families, too. This is what Sider is saying. If we can provide better access to clean water for people without them spending so much time getting water, and also help with disease control, people would be much more productive. Of course, there will need to be training and access to capital so people can buy animals, tools, and other supplies needed to begin businesses, too. There are several Christian organizations who help improve opportunities for the poor. This support may be in the form of a small loan or training. It can also be a safe way for poor people to save and build up capital. HOPE International, KIVA, SALT, and MEDA are some of these organizations who provide this type of ministry. I am not endorsing any of these but just making you aware that there are Christian organizations that help the poor in ways other than just giving them a handout.

Blomberg addresses a holistic approach to helping people, "If holistic salvation represents the ultimate good God wants all to receive, then our charitable giving should be directed to individuals, church-es or organizations that minister holistically, caring for people's bod-ies as well as their souls, addressing their physical as well as their spiritual circumstances."[5] This is good advice to consider when you are trying to decide where to give your time and money.

Since research shows that most Christians do not give 10 percent to their local church, does that mean you should give all your contri-butions to your home church if your church doesn't help the poor? Practically, with limited exceptions, I believe the first 10 percent should go to your local church, and if you feel led to do so, I believe giving all your contributions to your home church is just fine. But you may want to begin giving to organizations that help the poor by providing ways for the poor to begin helping themselves. Hope-fully your church is being given enough money to adequately fund the necessary operations of the church and to help the poor within your own church. If this is not the case, I believe some of your extra giving (above the tithe) should be given to the poor within your own church and also your own family as there is need. This could mean you won't take a tax deduction for all your giving, and that is ok. While I believe you should take advantage of all legal tax deductions possible, you should never make your ability to deduct the gift a requirement of giving.

Here are some practical guidelines for how to allocate your giving:

1. To your local church.

2. To the needy in your church, your family, and your communi-ty. Some of this giving could be to ministries who feed and/or house homeless people in your city.

3. To help the needy in our world.

4. To people with whom you have a relationship with and who are doing God's work in reaching the world. Our family gives some support to several missionaries. We do not support anyone we do not know personally. We have visited two of these mission-aries in the country where they minister. It was a way to help connect us and our children to where we give.

5. To organizations that minister to you. This could be radio stations and/or speakers on the radio, colleges and universities, museums, or other non-profits. If these organizations are ministering to you, they are probably ministering to a lot of other people who may not be able to give as much as you are able to give.

Other Giving Considerations

While I do believe a vast majority of us, and I mean 99 percent-plus, should give the first 10 percent to the local church, might there be some situations where this could be unwise? What if you make $1 million per year and attend a small church? Giving 10 percent would mean giving $100,000 to your church, which could be enough to fund the entire church budget. Would this be wise? Maybe and maybe not. I think this depends on the church leadership and whether giving that much makes the leadership feel uncomfortable. Assuming your church is good at setting maximums for itself and giving away what it doesn't need to help the poor, giving the entire tithe to your local church could work. But, if the church feels uncomfortable with this level of giving from one individual, or others in the church begin to feel like their own giving doesn't really matter anymore because the amount you give is so large, you might need to have a conversation with the elders of the church and decide how to handle your giving to the church. It could take the form of designated giving through the church. Be careful with this as designated giving can be a way to manipulate the church, too. Designated giving should always be to projects pre-approved by church leadership, not a way to force a church to give money to specific people or causes so you can receive a tax deduction. If there are needy people you know, help them! Don't just help them if you can deduct it off your taxes.

There may be rare situations when you feel called to stay in a church but the leadership of the church is not being godly and wise in how they handle God's money. Some people would suggest the way to create change is to withhold your money. I disagree. You need to talk with your church leadership and maybe even suggest bringing in someone from the outside to help guide the discussions. But withholding your support is manipulative and a way to exert power. I don't believe this is a godly attitude toward your leadership. If you continue to believe your leadership is wrong, leave that church and find one that is handling God's money well. Before you leave a church for this reason, get some outside counsel. It could be that you are not seeing things clearly and would just find the same "issues" at the next church and the next church, and so forth.

Another consideration about giving is whether substituting service for giving is valid or not. The Barna Group uncovered an interesting answer to the question: "Should volunteering at church substitute for tithing?" The paper (dated August 1, 2017), when asked if it is "okay" for members to volunteer for their church instead of giving financially, found that 85 percent of pastors strongly disagreed or somewhat disagreed. But the general Christian population, titled "Christians" by Barna, had an opposite response. Only 10 percent strongly disagreed, and 11 percent somewhat disagreed. Thirty-one percent of Christians were neutral on the topic and 47 percent of Christians strongly agreed or somewhat agreed that it was okay to volunteer instead of giving financially. Another interesting finding of the survey was that 77 percent of Christians who gave $2,500 or more annually to their church had also volunteered within the last month. It might be easy to speculate that pastors were just looking out for their own interests, but our money usually goes where our heart is. If we are truly invested in our church, both our money and our time will go there.

Should any of our extra giving above the tithe go to non-Christian organizations? While you will ultimately need to decide this for yourself, I strongly suggest the majority of a Christian's giving should go to Christ-based organizations. As Christians, our ultimate mission is to reach the world for Christ. While there are museums and other organizations that provide some value to society, these organizations would seem to fall into the same category as how Paul talks about physical training only having some value (1 Tim. 4:8). When we divert substantial giving to non-Christian organizations, we will not be able to as quickly fulfill our mission to reach the entire world for Christ.

Money and Marriage

When it comes to discussions about money within your marriage, they aren't always easy, whether those discussions relate to giving or buying other things. Most of us marry someone with some similar interests but who is extremely different in personality. So, we don't always agree. I tell my children that if it wasn't for their mother, the walls in our house would be really boring. I'm an accountant, and my wife is very gifted artistically. Some of our children have her artistic ability and some have mine, which is almost none. My wife likes to decorate, and it used to bug me because I saw money going onto our walls. But I have learned to appreciate her gift for making our house inviting and helping people feel comfortable when they visit. The same may apply to giving. One of you may have a really generous heart, and one of you may be more cautious. You need to learn to value the other spouse's perspective while still being honest with your own perspective.

My wife and I have a "contribution checking" account. After being married a couple of years and realizing we would get to Sunday and not have enough in our checkbook to give our tithe, we started doing what I now believe to be more biblical. We started setting aside the tithe when we got paid, not co-mingling it with the money we lived on. I believe this discipline fits better with the Proverbs 3:9 first-fruits concept and the 1 Corinthians 16:2 idea of setting aside an agreed amount of your income. Now we fund our contribution account each month with the amount we have agreed to set aside only for contributions. This includes both the tithe and the extra we set aside.

But we also give above this amount as we feel called to give. The amount in the contributions account is the minimum we give, not the maximum. My wife and I have given each other freedom to write checks out of this account for up to $50 each without consulting the other person if we want to give to a ministry. I know $50 might sound like a small amount, but we really try to do life together, including our giving. Maybe if our family income was $1 million per year, we would raise that limit, but maybe not. The $50 is a way we have some flexibility but are also forced to talk about giving. Conversations about giving are not always easy and we don't always agree. Recently we had some missionary friends who were leading a trip in another country and needed over $10,000 to fund the trip. Both my wife and I wanted to help. I was thinking of giving a maximum of $1,000, knowing our contribution account had almost nothing left in it for the year and we would be taking money out of another "fund" if we gave. When I talked with my wife, she said she wanted to give a minimum of $1,000 to help with the trip. We gave $1,000. Not all of our conversations on giving are that easy but we often are thinking about either the same amount or really close to the same amount. Sometimes we need to talk, wait awhile, and talk again because we just aren't very close to the same amount. In those moments, one of us is probably hearing the Holy Spirit and one of us isn't. Maybe neither of us is hearing the Holy Spirit clearly. So, we need to pray more about it and talk again.

This book isn't supposed to be a book on money and marriage, but, if you are married, you will need to decide how much to give and where to give. I really hope you do that together even if you need to get other people involved in helping you as you decide how much and where to give. I suggest an older couple from your church or your pastor and his or her spouse. My wife and I have done this a couple of times in the past. We seemed to be at a place of disagreement and couldn't get past it. We met with another couple and it really helped. They didn't tell us what to do but helped us understand each other better and get us past the roadblocks. Whatever you do, don't just disagree and not get help. We all need help at times in life. Satan tries to isolate us. Don't let Satan win that battle.

David Platt in his book *Radical* says, "I wonder if followers of Christ 150 years from now will look back at Christians in America today and ask, 'How could they live in such big houses? How could they drive such nice cars and wear such nice clothes? How could they live in such affluence while thousands of children were dying because they didn't have food and water? How could they go on with their lives as though the billions of poor didn't even exist?'"[6] It is a lot to think about and worth it. I hope this chapter has been helpful in this.

THINK AND DISCUSS

1. Do you believe Bono was correct to state that God is with us if we are with the vulnerable and poor? Do you currently give money to an organization that helps the poor?

   _____

   _____

   _____

2. Do you have or have you considered opening a separate contribution checking account? Do you believe this would help you be more purposeful in giving generously?

   _____

   _____

   _____

LIVING IT OUT

1. If you haven't already done so, open a contribution checking account. Fund this account systematically each month with the amount you plan to contribute both to your church and to other organizations, so you won't spend it on other things.

2. Research organizations that help the poor. Decide how much you can give them each month and start giving even if it is a very small amount each month.

14.
MAKING MAXIMUMS
A REALITY FOR
YOUR STAGE IN LIFE

As you have been reading this book, let's assume you want to begin using the concept of maximums but don't know where to begin. It can seem a little or a lot overwhelming. And we are all at somewhat different stages of living and giving. This chapter addresses the various stages in life and provides some suggestions on how to use maximums at the life stage where you find yourself and where to go in the future. Hopefully, you will find a stage similar enough to where you are now and can begin there.

There are a couple of essential concepts for us to grasp if we are going to find success in setting maximums, the first being that Christian giving, and all Christian stewardship, is the giving of self as to the Lord.[1] If we are still living for self rather than the Lord, we will not find contentment in setting maximums. Randy Alcorn says something similar, "I'm not saying that it's easy to give. I'm saying—and there are thousands who will agree—that it's much easier to live on 90 percent or 50 percent or 10 percent of your income inside the will of God than it is to live on 100 percent outside it."[2] It will be essential to give yourself totally to God to stick with the maximums you set. Otherwise, the stuff we can buy to supposedly "improve" our lives will begin to get into our hearts and we will not stick to a life of maximums.

The second essential concept is that we need to begin viewing money the way Jacques Ellul suggests, "We must bring money back to its simple role as a material instrument. When money is no more than an object, when it has lost its seductiveness, its supreme value, its superhuman splendor, then we can use it like any other of our belongings, like any machine."[3] Once we are able to grasp and agree to live by these two concepts, we are able to begin applying the following practices for setting maximums to our financial lives.

Pre-college Age

If you are young, I applaud you for reading this book and making it this far. It means you are feeling the Holy Spirit's tug on your heart to live a life of generosity. You have such a great advantage if you begin setting maximums for your life now. Most students come to college and admit their parents have not done a great job of teaching them about money, or their parents don't even manage money well themselves. Your parents might understand money very well but just haven't done a really good job of teaching you. They believe you will just learn by watching them. That method can work but just watching isn't the best teacher. If you don't feel very knowledgeable about handling money and your parents seem to be good at it, ask them to teach you more. If you don't feel comfortable asking them, pray about whether there is someone else you can ask. The Holy Spirit should bring someone to mind.

Begin to set limits on your own spending now. Spend time with your friends but decide how much money you are going to spend on food and drink each month. Set maximums on how much you will spend on clothes and shoes. If you don't have a job, I encourage you to get a part-time job for a few hours a week and tithe on your earnings. Begin thinking about education and what being educated will look like for you so you can earn a living during your adult life. As was explained earlier in this book, not everyone should go to college, but most people will. Begin talking to your parents about what education will look like for you and what you both can afford together. There is great value to a good Christian college education, as it will inform your thinking and worldview for your entire life, but you might not be able to afford Christian college for all your college career or even any of it. Going to a junior college, regional state university, or state university for a couple of years and then transferring to a Christian college might work well.

Don't get too worried about having all your maximums set right now. Begin to take steps. Think about the maximum type of car you will drive, maximum house, and so forth. Thinking about these things now will help you later. Take mission trips or at least one trip to a developing country. Seeing how other people live has really helped me and will help you know how blessed you are, even if other people in the United States seem to have much more stuff than you have.

The point is to begin thinking about what maximums will mean to you. I have in mind an amount I want to give away before I die—$500,000. I think my wife and I will get there and hopefully give more. I think it might be possible to give another $500,000 when we die for a total of $1 million. I hope it is more, but since we have a maximum retirement account balance, we might not make it to $1 million. If you are still a teenager, with inflation you will probably earn a lot more than I will earn in my lifetime and you could give away a lot more. Pray about it and set a goal.

Currently in College

Once you are in college and have a pretty clear understanding of your major, keep at it and finish as quickly as possible. Set maximums on how much money you will spend on recreation and entertainment, food, clothes, and so on. Make sure you have a job, as learning to use your time wisely is one of the most valuable skills you can take out of college, plus having a job will help minimize your college debt. Tithe on your earnings. Pray about how you will implement maximums after college.

If you are in a major where the earning potential after college is pretty low, consider whether any debt you are incurring now is necessary or if you need to transfer to a less expensive college or university. While I really believe Christian education is valuable, it isn't worth having so much debt that you can't afford to live on your own after college. When you graduate, resist the urge to begin life at the level where your parents are now financially. This means recognizing you will begin with used things or live without some things your parents now have. Remember they had twenty-five to thirty years to afford such things and you can get yourself into a trap trying to have nice things right away. You may choose to never have "nice" things compared to our culture and I applaud you for that.

If you choose a life of maximums, people will be critical of you. Mostly, they will criticize because they are fighting an internal battle, and if they can get you to change your thinking, they will feel better about spending money on themselves. If they admit your lifestyle of maximums has credibility, they have to consider that for themselves. If an entire Christian-college generation begins living by maximums, the world will be changed for Christ very quickly.

Post-college Age

If you are reading this and have recently graduated from college, meaning you are somewhere in your twenties, start paying off debt as quickly as possible while still tithing and giving extra as you sense the Holy Spirit guiding you to give. Unless you believe God is leading you otherwise, make paying off college debt your priority. I disagree with some financial advisors who say you should give only a tithe until you are out of debt. Let the Holy Spirit lead you on this. You might have a college friend who is headed toward the mission field and believe God is leading you to help support them.

Crown Ministries has some good material on getting out of debt. Dave Ramsey does too. I believe either is a good plan to follow as long as you don't allow the plan to become the most important thing in life. Focus on getting out of debt instead of getting a new car or buying other stuff you don't really need. Once you are out of debt, focus on saving for the down payment on a house if you plan to stay in the same town or city for several years and want to own a house. If you plan to move within a couple of years, buying a house will usually cost more money overall after you sell it and pay the realtor fee. If you buy a house, buy a modest one so you can pay it off quickly and then decide if you need a larger house. But you should already know what your maximum house will be and don't let promotions or bonuses at work change your mind unless you feel strongly that God is leading you to change your maximum.

Don't become fixated on money and make saving money into an idol. Most people in the United States aren't careful enough with God's money and some people become too consumed with managing money. You need a balance. You probably should start contributing to a retirement account if your company has one and matches contributions. If your company does not have a retirement account or does not match, consider paying off debt more quickly instead. This is a tricky decision. Remember that you can lose the money invested in financial markets and your debt will still be there. For most people, putting a limited amount into retirement while focusing on paying off debt is probably a good idea.

You need to spend time with people, and you will probably need to spend some money to do this. This could mean buying coffee or lunch for someone or spending money on entertainment to be with people. I believe spending money to be with people is something Jesus would have done and would do if He lived in our society. But there should be a budgeted amount you are willing to spend on this. That doesn't mean you never spend more in a month if you believe it is needed. Budgets are to be a guide; they shouldn't run your life. Also, be careful on spending money for entertainment you do alone. We have so many ways to spend time being entertained alone today and being entertained alone isn't often healthy. God created us for relationship. Focus your entertainment spending on being with people.

Set a budget for yourself. Again, Crown and Ramsey have some good tools and there are online tools you could use. I just use an Excel spreadsheet because it works for me. You need to track your spending and have some guidelines on how much you are wanting to spend in the different categories. Tracking spending is important for every age category.

Thirties and Early Forties

Much of the focus of this time of life is raising children. If you are single or do not have children and have set maximums for your lifestyle, you should be able to begin giving substantially more than the tithe while still contributing to retirement and buying a house. Randy Alcorn asks forty questions in *Money, Possessions, and Eternity* with question number 14 being, "Am I really in danger of giving too much too soon? Or is the only real danger giving too little too late?"[4] Be generous as God leads you.

When it comes to children, remember that God gives us good gifts, but we don't get everything we want nor do we have the same giftings as other people have. You are not hurting your children if they don't have everything their friends have. Here are a couple of things to think about: "Is it more harmful for children to share the experiences of the rich or the experiences of the poor? If the teaching of the Bible is taken seriously, the answer to this question must be obvious."[5] "For those of us who are wealthy, it is sobering to find in the Scriptures scarcely any record of repentance on the part of the rich."[6]

Prayerfully consider how much time and money to spend on recreational and club sports. I see families who are so concerned that their child will be left behind if the family does not invest in club sports. If you have a very gifted child in a sport, it usually shows up at a very young age and you can consider spending some time and money on the sport. Remember that Paul in 1 Timothy 4:8 says physical training has some value, but Paul doesn't say it has a lot of value. I see Christian parents putting physical training before Christian training. They have it backwards. Set maximums on how much time and money you will spend with your children on physical training and get them to Christian activities that will influence their lives far longer than the physical activity will. Just so you know, I was a three-sport athlete in high school and had a son run track and cross country during college, so I know how much time athletic training can take. Find a balance and set maximums.

If you are able, pay off your house and stay in it. Set a maximum on the type of house you will own and stick with that maximum. Don't be tempted by seeing other people your age buying nicer homes. If you believe my discussion on inheritance and how education today is a way to provide for your children's ability to provide for themselves, you may need the money you are paying for your mortgage now to help your children with college or trade school later; taking on more debt for a more expensive house will hinder your ability to help your children.

Hopefully you have been saving for vehicles instead of borrowing to buy vehicles. If you haven't been doing this, pay off your current vehicles and begin putting the payment into a bank account to save for the next vehicle purchase. It may mean you have older cars than your friends, but your goal is to increase your heavenly account and not have your reward now. "Are we excited about treasures in heaven?"[7] Don't allow nice stuff you could own today divert your focus.

Let your children know how you spend money and don't be afraid to tell them you have chosen to give money away rather than buy stuff for yourself or your family. Be careful to not say you don't have enough money to buy something you really could afford. But explain why you have chosen to not spend money on the item(s). Your children may not always agree with you or think that this way of spending money is fair to them. I have to remind myself often that I'm not after my children's agreement, but I want to set an example they will respect when they are older.

Help your children learn to manage money. There are different ways to do this. I'll share how we have decided to help our children, but I don't believe this is the only way. We pay our children monthly for the work they do. It is more like a salary than an hourly wage. Some parents pay for jobs and I believe that is perfectly fine. My wife and I have decided we will pay the same amount per month and deduct from the amount if our children do not complete the required tasks that month. Sometimes we give a little bonus if we have extra work during the month (like shoveling a lot of snow) but we don't always pay extra if we have more work. We are a family and sometimes we just have extra work. Most jobs your children will have after college will be salaried positions and they won't be paid extra for working more hours when the job requires more hours.

This payment system begins for each child when the child turns 10 years old and continues until they go to college. Each child is required to tithe on the amount they receive each month, to buy their own clothes, coats, boots, and so forth, and pay for any gifts they give to others. They also have to pay for recreational activities that go beyond youth group activities. We usually pay for church-related activities because we don't want our children to say they won't go to the church activity just to save money. We have purposely set the amount we give to the child each month low enough that they will want to find a job and work a few hours a week by the time they can drive. It isn't a perfect system, but it has really helped our children understand money and that there is a limited supply of money. Our children usually return from college after the first semester and talk about how other college students just don't seem to understand money.

It might sound like a contradiction to require our children to tithe on their earnings when I made this choice myself instead of keeping all of my birthday money when I was 10 years old. I believe there is a habit formed by doing something over and over, and I have decided I want to foster that habit in our younger children. Most of our children are now adults and we don't quiz them on whether they tithe and/or how much they give away. I hope their habit of tithing when younger has carried over to their adult years. I have one daughter who has continued to tithe during college and was shocked when none of her college friends gave any of their income to a church. I don't believe we become generous when we finally feel like we have a lot of money. Generosity is an attitude whether you are poor or rich; I doubt my daughter's college friends will begin to tithe or become generous just because they get a good job after college.

You have to allow your children to make some bad money decisions and help them learn from these bad choices. This can be hard to watch but stopping them from making a bad decision will probably not help them in the long run. If your child is continually making bad decisions, you may need to step in and help or set guidelines but only do this as a last resort.

Take your children on mission trips or find ways for them to go with a group. I like the idea of going with the child, if possible. This will allow you to share the experience and have reference points to talk about what they saw and learned after you get back home. I believe the best trips happen when your child is at least a teenager, but some children might be able to have a meaningful experience when they are younger.

If you are being exposed to thinking in maximums for the first time, you may need to start where the "soon after college" group is starting. Pay off debt as soon as possible. You might need to sell your vehicles and buy cheaper ones. You may need to quit taking such expensive vacations or take them less often and put the money toward paying off debt. Don't let Satan deceive you that starting now is too late. It is never too late to begin sowing into your heavenly account. Starting late is better than never starting.

Late Forties and Fifties

Often, the focus of these years is helping your children with college or a trade school. The key is providing them with what they need to be able to provide for themselves. Review the section on inheritance for a discussion on education. You may be in a position to borrow some money to help your children with education but make sure your children are invested in their education, too. One of the best ways your child can prepare for a first job and improve his or her resume is to work a job during college and take internships, that is if internships are offered for the major your child has chosen.

As a college educator, I am realizing fewer employers care about students being athletes during college and more employers want internship experience. College sports are becoming year-round activities, even at smaller colleges, for almost every sport, and coaches are becoming less willing to allow an athlete on scholarship to leave campus for a full-time internship. Unless your child is truly a star athlete in their chosen sport, he or she can probably make a lot more money working jobs during college for the same number of hours that athletes use to practice than they will receive in athletic scholarships. I believe being on an athletic team during college has some lifelong value but very few athletes receive more in scholarship money than they could make working a job. Help your children think through these issues and how they will help pay for the training they will need to provide for themselves as an adult.

If your child is uncertain of a career, have them take a career test to find out how their talents and personality fit in with people in different professions. Compared to spending a couple of wasted years pursuing a degree or profession they won't like, the cost of such a career test is cheap. Some colleges and universities offer these tests free or at a very reduced rate as the institution wants the student to graduate with a degree they like and, therefore, feel better about his or her educational experience. Don't be too concerned if your child changes his or her major a couple of times during the first couple years of college. It happens to a lot of students.

If you have avoided the temptation to increase your standard of living once your house has been paid for, you should be in a good position to both help your children with education and continue contributing to retirement. But, for some of you, your retirement account could be totally funded by sometime in your fifties. While you need to prayerfully consider this next statement, the possibility exists that you should stop putting money into your retirement account while your children are in college and help your children instead. If you agree that giving a large inheritance to your children after you die is not as important as making sure your children are educated, this will make sense. Financial advisors will not tell you this as it goes against most current investing advice. The issue is what is most important to you. Is it giving a lot of money to your sixty-year-old children when you die, or making sure they have the education necessary to provide well for themselves from the time they are in their early twenties until they are in their sixties?

Also, this time of life can be a very good income-earning time for you. Be generous with the money you don't really need to live on or to fund education and retirement. "Postponed giving is usually postponed obedience, and postponed obedience is disobedience."[8]

If the concept of maximums is new to you and your financial life is a mess, you will need to be realistic with your children on what type of education you and they can afford. You may need to sell vehicles and/or your house and buy something less expensive to get rid of payments so you can pay off credit card debt and help your children with their education. You probably will need to cut back on things you have become accustomed to buying, such as specialty drinks and lunches. As shown earlier in this book, doing so can generate a lot of money each year. You may be taking vacations you don't really need to take and have to cut out those expenses to generate cash flow. It will be hard but keep the end goal in mind. You are trying to deposit riches into your heavenly account instead of receiving all your reward in this life. "Either Jesus and his kingdom matter so much that we are ready to sacrifice everything else, including our possessions, or we are not serious about Jesus."[9]

Sixties and Retirement

While I will still have a couple of daughters in college (if they decide to attend college) when I am in my sixties, most of you won't. This time in life should be one where you can give generously both in your time and money. I remember a guest speaker at our church many years ago speaking about volunteering. I doubt the entire sermon was about this, but I remember the part where he said so many church members in their retirement years believe they have already given their time to the church and so they stop volunteering. It is in this time of life, when your children are no longer in your home, that you should be giving time to your church and to other organizations if you believe in their missions. You have much wisdom from living sixty-plus years and others need that wisdom.

The "wisdom" of this culture says the sixties are a time to spend money on yourself. You have been spending on your children and now you can start getting and doing things that you didn't do when you had the expenses of children and college. Kreider writes, "The teachings of Jesus on giving clearly show that the real measure of our giving is not how much we give, but how much we hold back for ourselves. As our incomes advance, we tend to hold back for ourselves money which will meet progressively less-urgent real needs."[10] I think there is value in doing some traveling and seeing God's creation. By bicycling across the United States many years ago, I was astounded by God's creation and it helped me in my spiritual walk. Going to Israel with my wife has also helped me tremendously in understanding the Scriptures and Jesus. But going to Israel three or four times probably won't help me much. I think the same is true with costly vacations when the goal is to be re-created. If we need to go to expensive places to be recreated, I think we are misusing God's resources and spending money on ourselves that could have been invested to gain riches in heaven. Platt provides us with a worthwhile warning, "I could not help but think that somewhere along the way we had missed what is radical about our faith and replaced it with what is comfortable. We were settling for a Christianity that revolves around catering to ourselves when the central message of Christianity is actually about abandoning ourselves."[11]

While you probably have done this already, have conversations with your children about the future and the inheritance you are planning to give them when you die. If you have a child who has not handled life well and is hoping your death will give them a financial boost, they will be able to come to terms with how they need to care for themselves now instead of hoping to receive a large windfall when you die or even hoping that you die soon. This type of mindset in Bible times was almost a sure way to lose your land and be sold into slavery.

I think Lynn Miller says it well, "I don't 'have it all' in financial terms, but I have sufficient money to worship with, meet my needs, and have some extra for more giving. And that's the key word in finding contentment: sufficiency."[12] During this time of life, we can be extraordinarily generous. "Generous people view their possessions as temporary; they are joining in a bigger story. Generous people are always looking toward the needs of others by using what they have been given. Things don't matter; people do. They open their houses to others. They open their pool for parties. They let people borrow their cars. They freely give, with no returns expected."[13] Use the money God has entrusted to you to gain friends in heaven as Jesus seems to teach in Luke 16. "Even generous Christians will look back on their lives and wish they had given more."[14]

There is no way to cover every individual situation, but my hope is that you found some ideas on how to begin putting a life of maximums into practice and what it will mean for each stage of your life.

THINK AND DISCUSS

1. Do you believe Randy Alcorn is correct in stating that it's much easier to live on 10 percent of your income inside the will of God than to live on 100 percent outside the will of God? Why or why not?

_____

_____

_____

2. What changes do you need to make today to begin making maximums a reality in your life?

_____

_____

_____

LIVING IT OUT

1. If you have not done so already, decide what changes you will make to begin living a lifestyle of maximums. Find someone else who can hold you accountable to make these changes.

2. Talk with other people you know who you believe would be interested in living by setting maximums.

CONCLUSION

C.S. Lewis says, "Prosperity knits a man to the world. He feels that he is 'finding his place in it,' while really it is finding its place in him."[1] Jesus warned against this very thing. When we put our treasure in things of this world, our hearts follow (Matt. 6:19–21). Setting maximums fights against the world finding its place in our hearts.

So, will you take part in this lifestyle of maximums? If you do, don't expect it to be easy. Expect to make a few mistakes during the journey. But also expect to find a lot of peace as the grip of our culture is released and you begin living for the future reward instead of the reward now. Doing this will not just affect you but it will have the power to affect future generations. What if more Christians started to live a maximums lifestyle and give more generously? Our world would be reached for Christ! Why hasn't the wealthiest society to ever live on earth already accomplished this? I believe it is mostly because we have been comfortable making this earth and the stuff we can enjoy here our home. Jesus said this world is not your home. Do we believe Him? I think we do believe, but we just like it here on earth. It is too comfortable for us. But it isn't this way for everyone on earth. The poor often have a much clearer eternal perspective than we generally do.

By setting maximums, we have already determined how much of this world we will let in, and we can keep material possessions and entertainment in its rightful place. We have chosen Voluntary Christian Socialism instead of allowing ourselves to be bought by the next pay raise or the next purchase that promises us a better life. We already have a better life. We understand the power of enough.[2] We can no longer be bought. Our bodies live in this world but our hearts are not consumed by the god of prosperity this world worships. We are free to give generously now because we know we are rich; we do not wait to be generous until we think we have finally become rich. "The good life is not found in luxury; rather it is found in a life that enhances the life of another human."[3] In setting maximums, we will find the good life.

THINK AND DISCUSS

1. Why do you believe the wealthiest society to ever live on earth has not accomplished the Great Commission?

_____

_____

_____

2. Can you become someone who enhances the life of other people? How? What is your motivation?

_____

_____

_____

LIVING IT OUT

1. What steps can you take today to give generously to someone in need?

2. Will you commit to a life of setting maximums?

RECOMMENDED RESOURCES
FOR FINANCIAL WISDOM

Crown Financial Ministries
crown.org

The Treasure Principle
by Randy Alcorn, Multnomah Publishers, 2017

Neither Poverty nor Riches
by Craig L. Blomberg, Eerdmans, 2000

Missions and Money (revised and expanded edition)
by Jonathan J. Bonk, Orbis Books, 2007

Money and Power
by Jacques Ellul, Wipf & Stock, 2009

Passing the Plate
by Smith & Emerson, Oxford University Press, 2008

The Christian Entrepreneur
by Carl Kreider, Herald Press, 1980

The Power of Enough
by Lynn A. Miller, Wipf & Stock, 2003

The Blessed Life
by Robert Morris, Regal, 2016

Radical: Taking Back Your Faith from the American Dream
by David Platt, Multnomah Books, 2010

Loving the Poor, Saving the Rich
by Helen Rhee, Baker Academic, 2012

Rich Christians in an Age of Hunger (6th edition)
by Ronald J. Sider, W Publishing Group, 2012

Fields of Gold
by Andy Stanley, Tyndale House Publishers, 2006

How to be Rich
by Andy Stanley, Zondervan, 2013

Jesus and Money
by Ben Witherington III, Bazos Press, 2010

NOTES

Introduction

1. C. S. Lewis, *The Screwtape Letters*, with "Screwtape Proposes a Toast" (New York: HarperOne, 2000).

2. Larry Burkett, *The Word on Finances* (Chicago: Moody Press, 1994), 113.

3. Randy C. Alcorn, *The Treasure Principle*, Lifechange Books (Sisters: Multnomah Publishers, 2001).

4. Jon Bonk, *Missions and Money: Affluence as a Missionary Problem*—revisited, revised and expanded ed. The American Society of Missiology Series, no. 15 (Maryknoll: Orbis Books, 2006).

5. Ronald J. Sider, *Rich Christians in an Age of Hunger: Moving from Affluence to Generosity*, 6th ed. (Nashville: W Publishing Group, an imprint of Thomas Nelson, 2015), 30.

1: Biblical Concepts of Money

1. David Platt, *Radical: Taking Back Your Faith from the American Dream*, 1st ed. (Colorado Springs: Multnomah Books, 2010), 19.

2. Christian Smith, Michael O. Emerson, and Patricia Snell, *Passing the Plate: Why American Christians Don't Give Away More Money* (Oxford; New York: Oxford University Press, 2008), 146.

3. Andy Stanley, *How to Be Rich: It's Not What You Have, It's What You Do with What You Have* (Grand Rapids: Zondervan, 2013).

4. Craig L. Blomberg, *Neither Poverty nor Riches: A Biblical Theology of Material Possessions, New Studies in Biblical Theology* / Eerdmans (Grand Rapids: Eerdmans, 1999).

5. Ibid, 165.

6. Sider, *Rich Christians in an Age of Hunger: Moving from Affluence to Generosity*, 83.

7. Blomberg, *Neither Poverty nor Riches*.

8. Ben Witherington, *Jesus and Money: A Guide for Times of Financial Crisis* (Grand Rapids: Brazos Press, 2010), 143.

9. John Piper, *Living in the Light: Money Sex & Power: Making the Most of Three Dangerous Opportunities* (Norhaven, Denmark: The Good Book Company, 2016), 60.

10. Mark Allan Powell, *Giving to God: The Bible's Good News about Living a Generous Life* (Grand Rapids: William B. Eerdmans Pub, 2006), 83.

2: How Fear Affects Our Use of Money

1. Robert T. Kiyosaki and Sharon L. Lechter, *Rich Dad, Poor Dad: What the Rich Teach Their Kids about Money That the Poor and Middle Class Do Not!* (Paradise Valley: TechPress, 1998), 37.

2. Andy Stanley, *Fields of Gold: A Place beyond Your Deepest Fears, a Prize beyond Your Wildest Imagination* (Wheaton: Tyndale House Publishers, 2004), 17, 56.

3. Robert Morris, *The Blessed Life* (Ventura: Regal Books, 2004), 50.

4. Stanley, *Fields of Gold*, 127.

5. Larry Burkett, *Dollars and Sense: What the Bible Says about You and Your Money* (Uhrichsville: Barbour and Company, 1993), 35.

6. Gary D. Moore, *End-Times Money Management: Protecting Your Resources without Losing Your Soul* (Grand Rapids: Zondervan Publishing House, 1999), 87.

3: Living by the Principle of Maximums

1. Larry Burkett, *Your Finances in Changing Times*, Moody Press rev. ed., The Christian Financial Concepts Series (Chicago: Moody Press, 1982), 88.

2. Platt, *Radical,* 128.

3. Jill Savage and Mark Savage, *Living with Less So Your Family Has More* (New York, Guideposts, 2010), 52.

4. B. Goudzwaard, H. M. de Lange, and Mark Vander Vennen, *Beyond Poverty and Affluence: Toward an Economy of Care with a Twelve-Step Program for Economic Recovery* (Grand Rapids: Geneva: W.B. Eerdmans Pub. Co.; WCC Publications, 1995), 159.

5. Josh Sanburn, "Minimalist Living: When a Lot Less Is More," Time.com, March 17, 2015, N.PAG.

6. Witherington, *Jesus and Money*, 131.

7. Sider, *Rich Christians in an Age of Hunger*, 106.

8. Alcorn, *The Treasure Principle*, 43.

4: The Relationship between Tithing and Maximums

1. "New Study Shows Trends in Tithing and Donating," Barna Group, April 4, 2008, https://www.barna.com/research/new-study-shows-trends-in-tithing-and-donating/.

2. "American Donor Trends," Barna Group, June 3, 2013, https://www.barna.com/research/american-donor-trends/.

3. "Christians' Financial Motivations Matter," Barna Group, June 13, 2017, https://www.barna.com/research/christians-financial-motivations-matter/.

4. Sider, *Rich Christians in an Age of Hunger*, 31.

5. Ibid.

6. Ken Stern, "Why the Rich Don't Give," Atlantic 311 (3), p. 75.

7. Sider, *Rich Christians in an Age of Hunger*, 193.

8. Howard Dayton, *Your Money Counts: The Biblical Guide to Earning, Spending, Saving, Investing, Giving, and Getting out of Debt* (Longwood: Crown Ministries, 2007), 142.

9. Lynn Miller, *Power of Enough: Finding Contentment* (Wipf & Stock Publishers, 2015), 26.

10. Dave Sutherland and Kirk Nowery, *The 33 Laws of Stewardship: Principles of a Life of True Fulfillment* (Camarillo: Spire Resources, 2003), 75.

5: How Maximums Relate to Our Standard of Living: Food, Clothes, Shoes

1. Sutherland and Nowery, *The 33 Laws of Stewardship: Principles of a Life of True Fulfillment,* 126.

2. Dayton, *Your Money Counts,* 12.

3. Wesley Kenneth Willmer and Martyn Smith, *God & Your Stuff: The Vital Link between Your Possessions and Your Soul* (Colorado Springs: NavPress, 2002).

4. Sutherland and Nowery, *The 33 Laws of Stewardship*, 135.

5. Stanley, *How to Be Rich*, 67.

6. Lynn Miller, *Power of Enough: Finding Contentment* (Wipf & Stock Publishers, 2015).

7. Jeff Shinabarger, *More or Less: Choosing a Lifestyle of Excessive Generosity,* 1st ed. (Colorado Springs, David C Cook, 2013), 36.

8. Sider, *Rich Christians in an Age of Hunger*, 94.

9. Nanci Hellmich, "Cost of Feeding a Family of Four: $146 to $289 a Week," USA TODAY, May 1, 2013, https://www. usatoday.com/story/news/nation/2013/05/01/grocery-costs-for-family/2104165/.

10. Witherington, *Jesus and Money,* 126.

11. Carl Kreider, *The Christian Entrepreneur,* The Conrad Grebel Lectures; 1979 (Scottdale: Herald Press, 1980).

12. Daniel M. Bell, *The Economy of Desire: Christianity and Capitalism in a Postmodern World, The Church and Postmodern Culture* (Grand Rapids: Baker Academic, 2012), 10.

13. Kim Pinnelli, "Average Cost of Clothing Per Month Will Surprise You," CreditDonkey, November 15, 2017, https:// www.creditdonkey.com/average-cost-clothing-per-month.html.

14. Utpal Dholakia, "How Much Are Your Shoes Really Costing You?" Psychology Today, October 20, 2015, https:// www.psychologytoday.com/blog/the-science-behind-behavior/201510/how-much-are-your-shoes-really-costing-you.

6: Housing and Debt

1. Stanley, *Fields of Gold,* 67.

2. Mark Perry, "New US Homes Today Are 1,000 Square Feet Larger than in 1973 and Living Space per Person Has Nearly Doubled," AEI, June 5, 2016, http://www.aei.org/publication/new-us-homes-today-are-1000-square-feet-larger-than-in-1973-and-living-space-per-person-has-nearly-doubled/.

3. Blomberg, *Neither Poverty nor Riches.*

7: Vehicles and Transportation

1. David Weliver, "How Much Should You Spend On A Car?", Money Under 30 (blog), February 1, 2017, https://www. moneyunder30.com/how-much-car-can-you-afford.

8: Possessions We Buy

1. Daniel Hillion, "Responsible Generosity," Evangelical Review of Theology 37, no. 1 (January 2013): 34–45.

2. Powell, *Giving to God*, 87.

3. Hillion, "Responsible Generosity."

4. Sider, *Rich Christians in an Age of Hunger*, 101.

5. Willmer and Smith, *God & Your Stuff*, 74.

6. Arthur R. Simon, *How Much Is Enough? Hungering for God in an Affluent Culture* (Grand Rapids: Baker Books, 2003), 26.

7. Alcorn, *The Treasure Principle*, 41.

9: Recreation and Entertainment

1. Simon, *How Much Is Enough?*, 84.

2. Kreider, *The Christian Entrepreneur*.

3. Sutherland and Nowery, *The 33 Laws of Stewardship*, 67.

10: Retirement and Investing

1. Dayton, *Your Money Counts*, 95.

2. Witherington, *Jesus and Money*, 151.

3. Moore, *End-Times Money Management*, 54.

4. Howard Dayton, *Getting out of Debt* (Wheaton: Tyndale House Publishers, 1986), 25.

5. Burkett, *Your Finances in Changing Times*, 52.

6. Stanley, *How to Be Rich*, 77.

7. Blomberg, *Neither Poverty nor Riches*.

8. Ben Gose and Emily Gipple, "Rich Enclaves Are Not as Generous as the Wealthy Living Elsewhere," Chronicle of Philanthropy 24, no. 16 (August 23, 2012).

9. Jacques Ellul, *Money & Power* (Eugene: Wipf & Stock, 2009), 105.

10. Alcorn, *The Treasure Principle*, 67.

11. Burkett, *Your Finances in Changing Times*, 107.

11: Inheritance and Education

1. Sider, *Rich Christians in an Age of Hunger*, 72.

2. Ibid, 73.

3. Kreider, *The Christian Entrepreneur*, 165.

4. Ibid, 166.

12: Planning for Financial Disasters

1. Randy C. Alcorn, *Money, Possessions, and Eternity*, rev. and updated (Wheaton: Tyndale House Publishers, 2003), 348.

2. Larry Burkett, *Your Finances in Changing Times*, Moody Press rev. ed. The Christian Financial Concepts Series (Chicago: Moody Press, 1982).

3. Platt, *Radical*, 123.

4. Blomberg, *Neither Poverty nor Riches*, 154.

13: Where to Give

1. Powell, *Giving to God*, 158.

2. Blomberg, *Neither Poverty nor Riches*, 199.

3. St. Demetrios Greek Orthodox Church Camarillo, Bono from U2 on Generosity, accessed December 13, 2018, https://www.youtube.com/watch?v=hgGp1O9gnQY.

4. Sider, *Rich Christians in an Age of Hunger: Moving from Affluence to Generosity*, 6th ed. (Nashville: W Publishing Group, an imprint of Thomas Nelson, 2015).

5. Blomberg, *Neither Poverty nor Riches*, 247.

6. Platt, *Radical: Taking Back Your Faith from the American Dream*, 1st ed. (Colorado Springs: Multnomah Books, 2010).

14: Making Maximums a Reality for Your Stage in Life

1. Alfred Martin, *Biblical Stewardship*, rev. ed. (Dubuque, IA: ECS Ministries, 2005).

2. Alcorn, *The Treasure Principle*, 64.

3. Ellul, *Money & Power*, 110.

4. Alcorn, *Money, Possessions, and Eternity*, 219.

5. Bonk, *Missions and Money*, 175.

6. Ibid, 169.

7. Alcorn, *The Treasure Principle*, 76.

8. Alcorn, *Money, Possessions, and Eternity*, 343.

9. Sider, *Rich Christians in an Age of Hunger*, 112.

10. Kreider, *The Christian Entrepreneur*, 160.

11. Platt, *Radical*, 7.

12. Miller, *Power of Enough*, 48.

13. Shinabarger, *More or Less*, 250.

14. Stanley, *Fields of Gold*, 112.

Conclusion

1. Lewis, *The Screwtape Letters*, with "Screwtape Proposes a Toast," 143.

2. Miller, *Power of Enough*.

3. Shinabarger, *More or Less,* 181.

ABOUT THE AUTHOR

Roger Stichter (M.B.A., D.B.A., C.P.A.) has been a professor of accounting for 21 years at Grace College and Seminary in Winona Lake, Indiana. In 2013, he was awarded the Indiana Outstanding Educator Award by the Indiana CPA Society and awarded the Alva J. McClain Excellence in Teaching award from Grace College in 2018. Stichter also worked as a CPA in public accounting, was the corporate controller for Miller's Merry Manor, and the CFO for White's Residential and Family Services. He lives in Winona Lake, Indiana, with his wife of 35 years, Jane. They have seven living children, three grandchildren, three children-in-law, one grandchild, and one child, Rebecca, who is already enjoying heaven.